Advance praise for *And What Do You Do?*

'Making the most of our talents is in part what effective career planning involves. But there's more to it than that. It's also about securing the quality of life we seek. This book will build the skills and confidence necessary to develop a portfolio career. This workstyle will become all the more accessible and realisable for the host of readers that I'm sure will devour this gem of a book. Fulfilment beckons...'

Paul Chubb, Non-executive Director and Policy Adviser, Careers England

'Yet again, Barrie Hopson, and this time with his co-writer Katie Ledger, has produced a highly relevant and fun insight into career development.

Portfolio working is a fast-growing way to manage one's career and it can be daunting to consider – but this practical, detailed and effortless guide shows just how it can be done. It's a must-read for all career professionals and their customers who want a step by step guide to progress from earning an income from various sources in an apparent unstructured way, to creating a satisfying and enjoyable way to self-manage their career.'

Vivienne Brown, President, Institute of Careers Guidance 2009

'Finally, a book that proves there's a new way of slicing the work pie – and it's here to stay. As attention spans shrink and the world spins faster, portfolio careers mean diversity for older workers, excitement for younger workers and fulfilment for everyone. Why have one boring job-for-life when you can have seve

Tanya de Gr̶u̶n̶w̶a̶l̶d̶ ̶a̶ The Guide
̶luates

D1136477

2674704

'We were all born with the creative potential to make a difference through our work to our families, friends and communities. *And What Do You Do?* is a practical, inspiring and necessary book that allows you to be the artist of your career – a must-read for all those who value diversity, fulfilment and creativity in their work.'

Steven D'Souza, author of Brilliant Networking *and Executive Fellow,*
IE Business School

'Corporates have long known the benefits of having multiple suppliers, securing diverse revenue streams and building a portfolio of assets that play to their strategic strengths. This book is a must-read for people who want to apply these same principles to their personal lives for careers that are rewarding both financially and personally.'

Bruce Lynn, Director of Server Business Group, Microsoft UK

'This is an important book for HR professionals as it highlights that we will need to change our relationship with employees if we are going to attract and retain the most talented people. We are going to have to understand how to manage temporary teams of specialists working on "projects" and this will mean that we will need to be much more flexible in our working arrangements and the types of contracts we can offer people. This will also mean a very different understanding of what we mean by a "company". The successful companies of the future will be populated by portfolio workers doing what they love doing.'

Roy White, Vice President, Human Resources, Sony Europe

'Katie and Barrie have produced a practical and inspiring book. It shows how people can follow their vocation, express it through many vehicles and do valuable work. It will encourage many readers to make a living by doing fulfilling work and also getting funding. *And What Do You Do?* will enable them to build on their strengths and achieve their picture of success.'

Mike Pegg of The Strengths Academy and author of
The Strengths Way

'*And What Do You Do?* is an excellent book packed with practical, common sense advice. The right balance is struck between developing the necessary personal and interpersonal skills and using modern technology to get ahead. The sections on networking, story-telling and personal brand are comprehensive and hit the mark. Well written and researched, this is a valuable resource for anyone embarking on a portfolio career.'

Andy Lopata, business networking strategist, co-author of Building a Business on Bacon and Eggs *and of* .... and Death Came Third!

'As a mature baby boomer, I have at least three jobs at the moment and all of these make me the person I am. Thanks to Hopson and Ledger's excellent book, I have found a positive way to express myself and keep "my story" consistent and relevant.'

John Cull, Mentoring Consultant for PRIME (Prince's Initiative for Mature Enterprise)

'Anyone who manages a business that relies on creative people knows that they sometimes have creative lifestyles too. This book is a must-read for the employer who realises that sometimes you can only have the best people by only having part of them.'

David Brain, CEO & President Europe, Edelman PR

'Finally, a book about other people that juggle multiple existences: what a relief! Barrie and Katie write well together and the book is just like the conversation they planned – light and interesting while offering some gems of advice.'

Dr Angela Carter, Occupational Psychologist, Institute of Work Psychology, University of Sheffield

'The term "portfolio career" is now common parlance, but this book makes practical sense of it and shows – in inspirational terms – how to construct one's own.

Professor Tony Watts, Founding Fellow and Life President, National Association for Careers Education and Counselling

And What Do You Do?

And What Do You Do?

10 Steps to Creating a Portfolio Career

Barrie Hopson and Katie Ledger

A & C Black • London

First published in Great Britain 2009

A & C Black Publishers Ltd
36 Soho Square, London W1D 3QY
www.acblack.com

A CIP record for this book is available from the British Library.

ISBN: 9-781-4081-1630-2

This book is produced using paper that is made from wood grown in
managed, sustainable forests. It is natural, renewable and recyclable.
The logging and manufacturing processes conform to the environmental
regulations of the country of origin.

Design by Fiona Pike, Pike Design, Winchester
Typeset by RefineCatch, Bungay, Suffolk
Printed in the United Kingdom by Cox & Wyman, Reading RG1 8EX

From Katie to:

David, and our 'angels' Olivia and Max, who remind me daily of what is really important.

My wonderful mother for helping me to pursue my creatively chaotic portfolio career.

My dad for being my dad.

From Barrie to:

Rosie and Toby, my grandchildren, as it was written largely with their futures in mind.

CONTENTS

Portfolio of acknowledgements

In the course of the 18 months or so that we've been working on this project, planning the writing, producing a synopsis, rewriting it a dozen times, interviewing people with portfolio careers, reading everything we could find on the subject (not much), finding an agent who would protect our sanity and our footwear, the one question that we have been asked the most is:

'Why are you writing this book?'

A Toni Morrison quotation came to mind:'If there's a book you really want to read, but it hasn't been written yet, then you must write it.'

Barrie is often asked why he never writes books on his own. His answer is constant: 'Where would be the fun, the bouncing off of ideas, the texts at midnight about a new insight, the continual learning about oneself and about the person that you are writing with?'

EL Doctorow said that writing is a socially acceptable form of schizophrenia. Well – the joy of writing with someone else is that there really *are* two of you. One of the thrills of writing this book has been that not only can our publisher fail to differentiate between which of us has written what but that *we* are also now confused.

In 1895, Jules Renard wrote: 'Writing is a way of talking without being interrupted'. He obviously never had a co-author. One of us hates sentences that have more than 10 words – and that end in exclamation marks! The other espouses concepts about grammar that precede the digital age – and does not like dashes.

Both of us have had successful careers as communicators and for the first time in history it's now possible to write a book that's more like a genuine conversation. Communication should always be two way. In the past, books were written, people hopefully read them, sometimes authors got a book review or two containing the reviewer's opinions and you might get the occasional letter sent to you via your publisher.

We've written this book around the 'project' of exploring the concepts and practice of portfolio careers and we've blogged on this subject for more than a year. We've floated ideas, got responses, found other people interested in the same project. We've learned from them, borrowed some thoughts and words, and invited people to contribute to the book itself.

We continue to blog, essentially to encourage the portfolio careers conversation and we would love to hear your stories, ideas and developments so do contact us at www.portfoliocareers.net.

Our conversations to date include those with:

Charlotte Howard, our agent, who also came up with the final book title, and who negotiated a publishing contract with Lisa Carden from A&C Black, part of the Bloomsbury Group, who encouraged us right from our first meeting, and gave us such positive and constructive feedback.

The authors, bloggers and organisations who have contributed to the book: Steven D'Souza, Seth Godin, Sir Ken Robinson, Penelope Trunk, Carole Stone, Oli Barrett, Tom Peters, David Brain, Marianne Cantwell, Carol White Llewellyn, Mike Scally, Andy Lopata, David Pilbeam, Hannah Morgan, Talentsmoothie and Slivers-of-time.

The 35 people with portfolio careers whom we interviewed in depth about how they live their lives, their highs and lows, their insights and questions, their humour and passion for the careers they are pursuing

That 'Crazy Deranged Fool', Hugh MacLeod, for allowing us to use his insightful and witty drawings and for being a great example of how to create a successful portfolio career. (Hugh's bio and details appear at the back of the book.)

Steve Clayton, who helped Katie to embrace her 'inner geek' and inspired a digital journey that's just beginning.

Kojo Boateng for his talent and creativity in designing our digital reality.

David McKee, the artist, illustrator and creator of Mr. Benn, for allowing us to use his wonderful illustrations for our chapter on multiple selves.

Silje Alberthe Kamille Friis, from Denmark, whose artwork also depicted this concept so beautifully.

Colin Pontefract for his psychometric advice, which contributed to the diagnostic instrument that enables people to assess their potential for a portfolio career.

Bernard Haldane, who died in 2002 at the age of 91, the pioneer of ideas about career development and the provider of educational tools that still are at the heart of most career programmes.

Peter Drucker, who long after his death inspires and continually amazes us with his insights and wisdom and from whom we quote copiously.

John Dammone, from Salvo's Restaurant in Leeds, who provided the restaurant example for Step 7.

Richard Papworth-Smith for his Mind Map.

John White, for his superb designs for the four career patterns and the 'energy pot'.

And the wonderfully generous, greatly talented encourager, Mike Pegg, who urged us to meet up as he thought we might get on…

Last, but definitely not least, Charles Handy, who wrote and talked about portfolio careers long before many people considered them to be a possible career choice. Barrie recalls a conversation with Charles in 1990 when he talked animatedly about portfolio careers as being a major career pattern for the future.

We think that future has arrived.

Welcome to your brilliant new career!

Introduction:

There is another way...

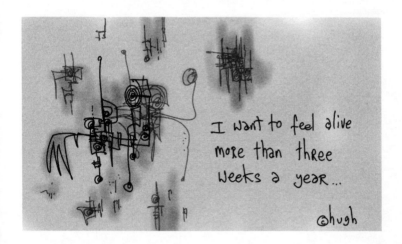

I want to feel alive more than three weeks a year...

@hugh

'A portfolio career is not the same thing as holding down three bad jobs and wishing you could figure out what to do with yourself. Rather, it is a scheme you pursue purposefully and positively, as a way to achieve financial or personal goals or a mixture of both.' Penelope Trunk[1]

'And what do you do?'

Do you dread that question? And how do you answer?

'I'm a plumber', 'I'm an accountant', 'I'm a teacher' – simple explanations of career choices. But what if you don't want to be defined by just *one* label? It's becoming increasingly common for people to say things like:

- 'I have three jobs. I'm a lawyer for several small companies, a professional cook and a food writer.' Hannah Miles

Or

- 'I work in a restaurant four nights a week, run a small shop three days a week and bake products for my husband's shop one day a week.' Veronique Jaquard

Or

- 'I spend three days a week working for a project for the elderly, one day doing admin for a charity, and two days building up my upholstery business. I love the different parts of me that get used by each of these activities.' Melanie

These are real people with real portfolio careers. The term was first mooted by management writer Charles Handy in the 1990s and essentially refers to a person doing *two or more different jobs for different employers*.

We've been discovering that hundreds, probably thousands and maybe even more than a million people have been, and still are, developing portfolio careers without being aware that this style of working has a name.

As for us? Katie has changed careers several times and always had 'jobs on the side'. From health-club management and software sales to personal trainer to trainee TV reporter; voice-over artist, BBC and ITN news reporter/presenter, communications consultant, conference host, business storyteller and now author. Barrie was a university lecturer who found it difficult to focus on just one job. He got funding for a research and training unit in the university, wrote books, created a publishing, training and consultancy business, left his 'secure' university job, set up a pizza company that folded, sold his company, bought back his old company, sold it again, now chairs one of its offshoots and has returned to writing books.

We differ in many ways. Social background, age, academic achievement, work experience, life experience and obviously gender. We share one important similarity though, and that's our attitude to change and risk. We both love learning new things and enjoy unpredictability.

A job is not for life – it's for however long it works for you. And our book is suggesting there is another way to find health, happiness and fulfilment in your work. It's not an easy option. It's good if you can multitask. It helps to have a strong support network. And persistence? Well, that's essential.

We both pursue portfolio careers at very different life stages – Barrie is in his mid 60s[2] and Katie considerably younger – yet this style of working has provided us with more satisfaction, fun and remuneration than any of the single jobs we've held. This book and our blog[3] promote portfolio careers as a very real option today with many pluses for individuals and also, we believe, for organisations.

Who have we written this book for?

It's primarily for people who are:

- employed but frustrated;
- employed but seeking a different work–life 'blend';
- starting out on their careers;
- self-employed or considering self-employment;
- unemployed but considering a return to paid work;
- retired but considering a return to paid work;
- juggling life commitments but wanting some paid work;
- portfolio workers.

Why have we written it?

Essentially, our aim is to answer the question we get asked so often: 'How do I create a portfolio career for myself?'

We think it all starts with how you view 'work'.

Does work have to mean 9 to 5, Monday to Friday? Does it mean going to an office/workspace a long commute from your home? Does it mean hard and fast hours, line manager, general manager, fixed holidays, pensions and benefits? Some of these can obviously be attractive but what happens when your job no longer exists, cutbacks have to be made or your company closes down? Are you in control? Or is someone else? What's your plan?

Instead of the much-publicised work–life *balance*, we prefer work–life *blend*. Balance suggests work and life are separate. You can do one or the other but not both at the same time. Blend suggests that work and the rest of life are not seen as equal and opposing forces but more of a coming together. A flexible approach where the sachets of jobs and life can be mixed in different amounts and in different ways. Some people will choose a blend with a heavier dose of paid work. Others will opt for more unpaid work. Some will focus on leisure activities and others their family commitments.

There is another way...

Think 'portfolio'. Think of your career as a 'portfolio of work' or 'portfolio of projects' that interest you and play to your skills. Forget job titles. You can literally think of it as a portfolio – carrying around with you all the skills and abilities you need to be able to design the life that you want for yourself.

'Our work may still largely define who we are, but our employers no longer will. Our sense of stability and our sources of encouragement, learning and growth in our careers will come from communities of practice and our engagements with like-minded peers who we meet and keep in touch with online, and not necessarily our long-term employment relationships. Rather, the people we meet at work join

the personal networks we create as we move from organisation to organisation over the life span of our careers.'[4]

Every job is now 'temporary'

This was increasingly the case even before the latest recession but few people now believe that any job is secure. That's a scary prospect for many, but it can provide opportunities too. The 'job for life' model is largely extinct, so 'security' now comes from being marketable and having transferable skills. As management expert Peter Drucker put it:

'Corporations once built to last like pyramids are now more like tents... You can't design your life around a temporary organisation.'[5]

When you're thinking about jobs, visualise a coin. On one side, it says 'job security'. But on the other, it says 'dependency'. Many people in full-time jobs don't realise that the price they pay for so-called job security is dependency.

New technology has transformed the world of work and provides many different career options and lifestyle choices. The futurist Anne Lise Kjaer predicts:

'Within a few years, the very phrase 'going to work' will be meaningless: work will be what we do, not a place we go to.'[6]

Economic security no longer exists unless you create it. Having multiple income streams can be a way of ensuring financial security. Risk is minimised because you're often dealing with several employers, so if the relationship with one employer ends, the cost isn't too high.

Flexicurity

The Slivers-of-time movement[7] talks about developing 'flexicurity':

'This is where security is not resting on a relationship with one organisation but on the sheer depth of experience and resourcefulness an individual has acquired by engaging with a much wider universe. As organisations increasingly face change, they may even prefer recruiting these multi-faceted individuals to promoting one more Company Man.'

You can choose the portfolio career option and do it full time, part time or for just a few hours now and then. You might be employed but will have at least two employers. You could be self-employed – as many are.

We've interviewed people from a wide variety of backgrounds and also discussed the issues with a number of businesses. People who've made this step include:

- Nick Beadle, a highly experienced lighting designer in theatres and who travels the country setting up lighting systems for new productions. He is also a professional photographer with a wide range of clients. His most recent venture has been to get trained to become a Reiki practitioner and he has just launched himself in this new career alongside his other work interests. And what do all of these jobs have in common? In a nutshell: Nick. He has too many interests to want to spend all of his working time with one employer and to focus on one range of work activities.

- Michelle Roughan, an events director for a financial services company and a Pilates instructor. She works three and a half days a week in the corporate world and two days for her own Pilates business. Most clients want general fitness, strength and flexibility but she also has a more specialised clientele who have multiple sclerosis, Parkinson's disease and breast cancer. She says, 'I love doing both jobs. I think I give more to both because I do the two.'

• Lamorna Trahair, 24, is one of four directors of the League of Adventurists, a 'not just for profit' travel company which helps raise money for charity. She organises events such as the London to Mongolia Mongol Rally for small, underpowered cars and an auto-rickshaw event in India. She's also a sought-after speaker and regular panel member for Gen Y[8] issues. Before that, she worked for the Volvo Ocean Race, had numerous jobs with different sailing teams and worked for a sports TV production company. She says:

'Get stuck in, pester people for a job. Persistence is never a bad thing. You have to be determined and passionate. The portfolio approach is scary and hair raising sometimes but really exciting and challenging all the time. You can't get complacent. I always have more than one project on the go. I can't imagine working any differently'.

• Zulfi Hussein, who after a long career in BT, now works for them on a project basis. He launched and part-owns a lifestyle management and concierge service. In addition, he's CEO of Global Synergy Solutions, which provides a wide range of business solutions, professional services and training and development. He's an author, a poet and a speaker in the areas of coaching, mentoring and diversity. He's also the founder of the Global Promise Foundation, a 'not for profit' organisation that brings together businesses to make a positive contribution within local communities with the aim of widening participation, particularly among ethnic minority and disadvantaged groups. (Not surprisingly, Zulfi has received many awards and in 2008 he was awarded an MBE for his charitable contributions.)

What do these people have in common? The answer is that they've all had difficulty finding a single job or even a career that used all of their skills in ways that were consistent with their values. They've all found, as indeed have the other people we've interviewed for this book, that **'there is another way'**. There is an alternative to the 20th-century dream of finding 'the one job that is right for you'. For many people that dream has become a nightmare.

Not everyone wants to spend all of his or her paid working hours doing the same thing in the same place in the same context for the same employer. In fact it's a bit odd historically for so many people to spend most of their time doing pretty much the same kind of thing. Before the Industrial Revolution, most people had a variety of daily and weekly tasks. In other parts of the world – India and Pakistan, for example – it's quite normal for the majority of people to have more than one job whether through choice or family pressure.

So a portfolio career is about doing two or more different jobs for different employers. The jobs might be totally unrelated or very similar or somewhere on the continuum. Sometimes the strands of a portfolio career even rotate seasonally: one of our interviewees, Lisa Milnor, is an accountant in Yorkshire in the summer and she runs a ski/chalet holiday business in France during the winter months:

'You are conditioned to want a career ladder but you get to a stage where you don't need that any more. I felt I was dying as a person inside.' Lisa Milnor (chalet holiday business in France/accountancy business in Yorkshire/ mentoring in Yorkshire)

So, how many jobs should you have? Well, we've mainly interviewed people with between two and five jobs – but for some people that's not enough. Trish Cowie, for example, has eight jobs (take a deep breath!):

- Age Concern – physical activity co-ordinator (25 hours a week)
- Salisbury District Council – sports and community officer (7.5 hours a week)
- Wiltshire Fire & Rescue Service – fitness advisor (about 6 hours a week)
- NHS Wiltshire – cardiac rehabilitation instructor (2 hours a week)
- Bikeability – national standard cycling instructor (about 1.5 hours a week)
- Action for Charity – freelance steward (20 days a year)
- Walking for Health – cascade trainer (6 days a year)
- Salisbury Hospital – bank fitness instructor (when required)
- And in her spare time, she is completing a course to become a lifeguard...

Trish says, 'The nice thing is that I don't get up each morning and think I have to go to work'.

People who opt for this workstyle like it because it gives them variety. Also, they don't have all of their career 'eggs' in one basket. If one job gets boring, they can focus more on the other ones or indeed even ditch the boring one. If they lose one job, they have other revenue streams to rely on.

A portfolio career gives legitimacy to people who have diverse interests and talents and want to express them. In the past, some people have been suspicious of individuals who have a reputation as 'a jack of all trades'. These comments typically have emanated from people who enjoy pursuing what we call 'single track careers' (see page 21). Interestingly, Bruce Lynn of Microsoft, in a response to one of Barrie's postings on our blog, said, 'I have always advised that portfolio players rather than being "jack of all trades and master of none" should look to be "jack of many trades and master of some".'

These people are now embracing the 'portfolio career' label with relief, finding in it a term which legitimises how they want to live their lives.

'I currently have at least three roles which are a mixture of working in corporate life, education and writing. Because of this I face many challenges such as managing my time, working harder to produce results in a shorter time frame and nurturing relationships which are more fluid with short connection opportunities. The blessing is that I have a rich perspective on different industries, feel intellectually stimulated and can bring valuable insights by looking for connections between the three areas of work.' Steven D'Souza

When asked to comment on the Vodafone Working Nation Report of 2008, David Molian of Cranfield University School of Management[9] stated that portfolio careers were a rapidly growing development on the working scene:

'Some people see it as bad thing, an erosion of the bedrock of loyalty on which British companies were once built. Others see it as a positive thing – a free market that encourages achievement, success and growth. I believe strongly that we will see this trend increasingly in the UK workplace, but most significantly within the entrepreneur community.'

Some fields of work – such as the arts, academia and consultancy – naturally lend themselves to portfolio careers. But we've been discovering people from all backgrounds who are now beginning to explore this option. We've even discovered portfolio careers among NHS doctors. Some we found were doing GP work and paid church activities, others were combining it with farming and one wrote magazine articles and novels (non-medical).

What are the facts?

- **1 million+ have two or more jobs.** There are 1.15 million people with two or more jobs. Of these, 65 per cent say they work in this way out of choice and not necessity.[10]

- **4 million are self-employed.** Since 1988, self-employment in the UK has more than doubled to close to 4 million with 30 per cent of those working part time.[11]

- **13 million+ would like part-time work.** 13.7 million people have said they would like to 'sell their hours' around other life commitments at some point each year in the UK.[12] Many of these, albeit unknowingly, could well be taking their first steps towards a portfolio career.

In addition, 60 per cent of new businesses now are started up in the home and home businesses account for more than a quarter of the UK's employment. As Ian Bushby, head of start-ups at BT Business, has commented, 'One interesting trend picked up by BT's Home Business Report 2008 found an increase in spare time start-ups, with a third of people running a home business in their free time. This thriving 5pm to 9pm economy offers would-be entrepreneurs a low-risk route to starting their own business while still retaining a regular income stream from their full-time jobs.'[13]

We don't know for sure how many of these people are pursuing portfolio careers, but many of them will be.

As we go to press, research from Accenture shows that almost 50 per cent of business professionals around the world believe they are insufficiently challenged, despite being confident of their skills and capabilities.[14] In a survey of 3,600 professionals from medium to large organisations in 18 countries across Europe, Asia, North America, South

America and Africa they found that 46 per cent of women and 49 per cent of men said they're not being challenged significantly in their current roles, yet more than three-quarters (76 per cent) of all respondents are confident of their skills and capabilities. No wonder people are realising that it's very difficult to satisfy all of one's work needs in just one job.

Who might be attracted to portfolio careers?
'The chronically under-aroused, corporate misfits, creatives.'
Chris Nel (consultant, diving instructor, army adviser)

That's the brilliantly idiosyncratic view of one of our interviewees about portfolio careers but we would paint a much broader picture. We would identify:

1 People starting out on a career and unsure about a long-term direction. It can be a way of 'trying on' a number of different types of paid work. Daniel Gilbert, author of *Stumbling on Happiness*[15] says the best way to figure out what will make you happy is to try it. Careers experts increasingly are encouraging people to experiment, test out possibilities, try it for size and make their minds up from actual work experience rather than trying to anticipate it all beforehand.

Marianne Cantwell[16], a highly experienced career change coach who works largely with Generation Ys says:

'Gen Y professionals report that all too often they suffer from the "too young" syndrome – brought on by a lack of role models. Many portfolio workers, independent consultants, or those who start their own businesses, appear to be much older. When young aspiring portfolio workers seek advice from more senior people within their industry, they speak (by default) to people who are living a single-track career, or to recruiters whose experience is of filling full-time roles. These people tend to say that anything other than single-track working is "too difficult" and certainly not viable for someone in their 20s.

Then when they get to their 30s and 40s they are conversely fed messages about being "too old". They now have "too many responsibilities", they are doing nicely on a regular career track and so are discouraged to risk "what they have achieved" and leap into a portfolio lifestyle.'

Generation Y workers, the new e-lancer generation – those born between 1981 and 1995 – are already demanding flexibility, development and learning opportunities, and increasingly they're bringing a social conscience to work. In the US, the Electronic Recruiting Exchange is reporting that as many as a third of new entrants to the workforce are looking for alternatives to full-time, single-track employment.

In an investigation into what 'Generation Y' wants from the workplace, TalentSmoothie[17] gathered data online from 2,521 survey participants. They found that Generation Y:

- wanted a job that uses their strengths with personal development seen as central;
- were most likely to resign if they weren't excited by their job or weren't developed in it;
- wanted to be trusted to get on with their own work;
- preferred to learn from peers, through coaching and mentoring, and through multi-sensory experiences. Recruitment based on their strengths resonated best with this group.[18]

2 People who have other responsibilities to work around, e.g. caring for children or other relatives.

'What many (people)... want is not more life and less work but a better balance of the different types of work', Charles Handy[19]

3 Many **over 50s** see it as a real alternative to the traditional 9 to 5 work style as the majority of this age group wants to continue in paid work but mostly they don't want more of the same.

'Project work is a great model for late middle age. It's not as intense. It leaves time for thinking about other items and projects. It's all about the C word – choice.' Richard Maude, 57 (video producer, consultant, mentor)

4 An increasing number of people are interested in **setting up their own business** but don't want to risk giving up their existing jobs completely. They can experiment with doing other jobs in their spare time or dropping down to part time and then trying on other jobs for size.

5 People with disabilities can find flexibility that could be more difficult in a single-track career. See the Slivers-of-time reference on page 5. Slivers-of-time doesn't exist in all parts of the country but it's worth checking their website to see if it exists near you.

Portfolio working can be a combination of traditional employment, contract work, temporary jobs, freelancing and self-employment. It can be a great way of developing a personal and professional 'brand' unique to you. Many of our respondents have discovered they can earn more money from three or more part-time jobs than from one full-time job, although, sadly this is not guaranteed!

Why is portfolio working becoming more popular?

An online poll of over 2,000 adults by The Skills Commission reveals that people spend nearly five years in jobs that don't make the best use of their skills. Twenty per cent of people are currently in such a job. Most people want to do work they love and feel passionate about, but sometimes despair they'll ever find it from one job or career. With the large increase in flexible working, it's increasingly possible to do many kinds of work in the same work year, work month, work week or even in the same day. Research conducted by Middlesex University[20] suggests more and more people are looking for exactly that.

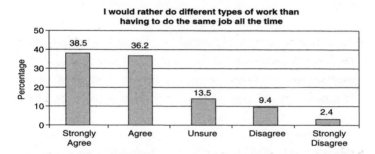

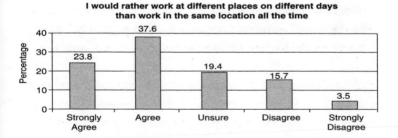

People are living and working longer, which gives us all more opportunity to create the paid workstyle that is right for us. As we age, we demand different things from our work and a single employer often can't provide us with the flexibility that we demand.

Sometimes the 'dailiness' of everyday life paints over the dreams we once had or have yet to come. Portfolio workers regularly tell us that having more than one job enables them to fulfil more of their dreams.

Hugh Macleod is a witty and talented artist, author, blogger, consultant, and marketer. His drawings always make us think, laugh or both and he was kind enough to let us reproduce some of our favourites in this book. He has this perspective:

'My paternal grandfather was a Scottish Highland crofter – he lived on a croft i.e. a very small holding of land, where he raised sheep and grew potatoes. I used to spend my summers there as a boy. We were very close. Crofting is a good life, but not a very financially rewarding one. It's very self-sufficient, though. The interesting thing for me, looking back, is that crofters never did 'just one thing'. Every day they had something else going on. One day it might be sheep. The next it might be a job working on the roads for the local council. I knew one crofter who drove the mail van. Another who ran the local post office. They would do their jobs, but after work they'd still have their sheep, cows and potatoes to attend to.

As my dad is fond of reminding me, I seem to have inherited the crofting mentality. I DON'T LIKE waking up in the morning and doing the same thing every day. I LIKE having all these different balls in the air – cartooning, painting, consulting, writing, marketing, blogging etc. Sure, part of me would like nothing better than just 'retiring to the desert and making paintings', but another part of me likes all the running around in different directions. And all this running around DOES get tiring, I can tell you that. Sometimes I LOVE the feeling of being constantly overwhelmed. Other times I utterly despise it.'

The pluses of a portfolio career

Our interviewees and the few research studies carried out on this group show that a portfolio career has many advantages.

- You're ultimately your own boss even if you're working for half a dozen different organisations.

'Having this way of working makes me different and I like that.'
Helen (education advisor and consultant, regional subject advisor, link tutor, method tutor, supply teacher, exam marker)

- You manage your own career and aren't dependent on organisations doing it for you.
- You enjoy a type of freedom when deciding when not to work.
- You can balance your paid and non-paid work.
- You have relative freedom from corporate agendas and politics.

'I would like the relative safety of a company life but it can't fulfil all my needs. I need to have the flexibility to change – the freedom to drop stuff and start something else.' Chris Nel

- It can allow you to implement the unique combination of strengths that only you have. If you have very contrasting work needs, it could be well nigh impossible to find a single job that will enable you to satisfy them all.

• Some psychologists argue that each of us has a number of 'selves' that co-exist, sometimes harmoniously, sometimes in competition. Having more than one job gives us greater opportunities to play and 'try on' the different aspects of ourselves.

• You can follow multiple passions.

'The different elements mean that you push yourself and you learn more things than if you just have one job. Having a range of jobs means that you can find out which you are most comfortable in doing.' Veronique Jaquard (restaurant *maître d'*, shopkeeper, bookkeeper and administrator for family business, patisserie chef)

• You're driven by the need for personal growth and fulfilment.
• The pace and constant change.
• It's often easier to say 'no' to a request or demand than when you have only one job and one boss.
• The excitement and unpredictability that can accompany this workstyle.
• There can be more leisure time.
• It can enable you to spread the risk, allowing you, for example, to earn money from one area while building up a new business or activity in another.
• Many portfolio workers have told us that things they have learned or experienced in one of their jobs has spilled over to benefit their contributions to their other jobs.
• 'It can help you to stay faithful to your partner.' This emerged when Barrie was talking to a woman with a portfolio career as

an art therapist, elected councillor, prospective MP and charity worker. She said, 'in theory, because you're all over the place, you probably have more opportunity to have an affair. But in practice this style of working means that even if you considered it, you're always too knackered to make it happen!'

The minuses of a portfolio career

'You can do anything you want – but not everything.'

Oli Barrett[21] (connector, writer, entrepreneur, organizer of speed networking events, speaker)

• There are huge pressures to manage your time to accommodate your different jobs.

'Every part of me is picked on…I go to the toilet and the phone rings…you have to listen at any time of the day or night.'
Heather Jackson (managing director of Believe Corporate Relations, strategic business and marketing consultancy)

• You may well have to invest considerable time and effort in marketing yourself.
• Initially, there are often real financial risks until you've acquired your portfolio. There can be a loss of employment benefits, such as pensions, health care, paid holidays, childcare, etc.
• You may be unwilling ever to turn down work offers.
• You may accept less desirable work because of financial uncertainty.[22]
• Sometimes there can be a lack of a regular routine along with feelings of isolation.

- You have to be able to do what some people call multi-tasking,[23] although in fact that means being able to switch between doing many things in quick succession.
- There may be greater pressure on immediate family for support.
- You may well work primarily on your own and not be part of a team.
- You now have to apply for a number of jobs and find employers willing to accept your chosen workstyle.
- You may have to sacrifice specialising, advancement and/or seniority and may find yourself 'managed' by less competent, less experienced people.
- Sometimes people won't understand what you're doing and will assume the workstyle you have is less socially valuable than having a single-track career.

'It doesn't feel like a proper job.'
Rob Butler (media consultant, magistrate, prison monitor)

The pluses of portfolio working for employers
- The number of people in part-time jobs has risen by almost 50 per cent since 1992 to 7.47 million. Part-time workers are often more attractive to employers, especially small businesses, as they offer more flexibility. For example, not every small business needs or can afford full-time marketing staff, HR functions or financial services.
- People also spend less and less time in any one job. In the US, the average time most workers spend in a job is 4.5 years. Generation Y people in particular tend to move on quickly.
- 3.5 million people now work from home – that's one-in-eight of the UK population; an increase of 600,000 since 1997.
- One third of British workers now work outside traditional hours.
- Recruiting portfolio workers could, in theory, eliminate overtime payments.

• As the business changes and develops, companies want people
  with different skills and talents. Seth Godin describes this well in a
  video interview with Katie, which you can see on our blog.[24]

There are other kinds of career

We believe there are four major career patterns:

Single-track career   Serial career   Lifestyle career   Portfolio career

Do you recognise these?

A single-track career is the one that many of
us have been brought up with. It developed with the
Industrial Revolution and the notion of specialisation.
Production was broken down into specific tasks and
people were employed to carry them out. The ladder
symbolises this track very well as we were all supposed
to be motivated to 'get on', meaning upwards. We
continued until gold watch time and then became a
retired teacher, builder, manager, shop worker, etc. If
we worked well and were loyal, we were promised
a long-term job and that we would be 'looked after'.
Careers advisors throughout the 20th century helped
young people to work out what they wanted to do for
a living. By this they meant finding the job and the
career that those young people would want to pursue
for the rest of their lives.

Pluses? You got security, opportunities to be trained and developed, a
predictable income, a feeling of belonging, recognised social status in that
everyone knew what you did and where you worked. You had a job title.

Minuses? Today, no organisation can offer a career or a job for life. Organisations are born and die or are reinvented, so there's no secure edifice against which you can lean your ladder. People themselves now change more quickly. The different generations want different things from work. Generation Y want personal development, work that reflects their social values and project work with people they respect. They are under no illusion that any position will last for more than a few years. Even the Baby Boomers in a recent survey[25] stated that they weren't sure what they wanted to do when they grew up. Forty-six per cent of them were looking forward to a new career that would be more satisfying than what they had previously had. Sixty-one per cent of them wanted to learn new skills.

Single-track careers are still possible but less so than they used to be – and job swapping between organisations is now often the only way of developing that work style.

A serial career is symbolised here by a chequerboard, which shows that people can move upwards, sideways, maybe downwards,

diagonally and so on. People who like periodic change favour this work style. Some individuals, no matter what they're doing or how successful they've been, just need to change every few years. They get bored and need to move on. They enjoy learning new skills and working in new environments. In the past they might have been characterised as feckless, a dilettante or unreliable. They get very involved in a job or a career but don't see it as something for life.

Pluses? You can experiment with a number of different jobs and careers. You choose your paid work according to what interests you, as opposed to what might help get you promotion or more money. You will need to develop what Sliversoftime call 'flexicurity'.

Minuses? Some people may view you as someone who 'never settles down'. You may never achieve seniority in an organisation.

A lifestyle career is most apparent at present in Generation X, although it's certainly visible in the other generational groups. Barnaby works three

days a week for a local authority and spends two days a week bringing up his two young children. Pam, his wife, also works three days a week (for an international oil company) and spends the other two days a week with their children. On only one day a week do the children go to a child minder. Barnaby and Pam are both clear that 'you only get one chance to bring up and enjoy your kids and we're not going to miss out on that'. Consequently, any major career progression or job changing will be put on hold until the children

are both at school. They will then review where they are and maybe make some career changes at that point. Barnaby is more likely to move on, as at heart he is actually a serial careerist. Pam is more likely to seek advancement in the company, as at heart she is a single-track careerist.

What we're finding is that the work–family dimension is not the only factor promoting this work style. Some people wish to travel, do voluntary work abroad or return to being a student. In later years the work–family dimension may appear again with older relatives who need to be cared for. Apparently women now spend more time caring for one or both parents than they do bringing up their own children. Other people want an undemanding job that pays for them to pursue a hobby which can't support them financially or that they don't choose to support them. John works in a shop for six hours a day. It doesn't excite him or give him much satisfaction but it demands little from him. When he's home, he devotes most of his time to his garden and his bee keeping. The balance works for him.

Pluses? The opportunity to combine a range of paid and unpaid work that's important to you. Paid work doesn't dominate your life. You have a more balanced style of life. You can always shift into a different career pattern if your lifestyle changes.

Minuses? Career advancement is likely to suffer. Promotion can be seen as a headache rather than an opportunity. Financially there may be a price to pay, as even today it's not always possible to get a part-time job with the level of flexibility that's required.

A **portfolio career** is, of course, what the rest of this book is about.

Some commentators argue that it's possible to have a range of work styles and stay in the same organisation.[26] So, you could embark on a single track, start a family and become more lifestyle oriented, then discover some new possibilities in the organisation and become a serial careerist. You could only be a portfolio careerist, however, by having one of your jobs in that organisation.

Some people also move into and out of a portfolio career. Helen, a teacher, wanted a different challenge. Leaving her full-time teaching job, she took on a number of different jobs. She spent two days a week supporting staff in schools through coaching and mentoring, one day a week supply teaching, and one day a week supporting students on a PGCE course at Leeds University. She also spent time each month working for her professional association and then did examination marking during the summer. After a couple of years she opted to try out a full-time job again but after five weeks in her outdoor education role realised she'd made a mistake, on both a personal and professional level. She was then able to go back to the work with her subject professional body, supply teaching and PGCE work. As we write this, Helen is happy back in full-time employment once more (with an education authority) although interestingly she has 14 schools as her clients and they each have their individual issues. That must be about as close as you can get to pursuing a portfolio career within one organisation.

As well as choosing a preferred style of working – a career pattern, we also choose the context in which we work and how many hours we want to spend in paid work. The table below shows the relationship between these.

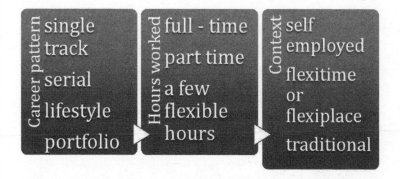

Career pattern	Hours worked	Context
single track serial lifestyle portfolio	full - time part time a few flexible hours	self employed flexitime or flexiplace traditional

So, you choose your preferred career pattern, then decide how much paid work you want to do, whether or not you'd like to do this as a self-employed person, or whether to negotiate flexitime or flexiplace arrangements with your employer. You do, of course, still have the traditional 9 to 5-ish work context as an option.

How do you create a portfolio career? The 10 Steps

Where to start? It's a bit like making a cup of tea: what do you put in first? Water, tea, milk or sugar? We're sure there's a scientifically proven way to make a perfect cup of tea but our point is it doesn't matter where you start, just as long as you actually begin somewhere. So we present the 10 Steps in what seems like a logical order to us, but if that doesn't work for you, start with the step that does.

Portfolio careers can be messy, confusing and chaotic. This is OK. Indeed it's necessary because out of the chaos will come some sort of order that is right for you – your unique portfolio of skills, values and selves.

Step 1 My portfolio career: Is it for me?

Step 1 has a questionnaire that will help you to decide if this workstyle is for you.

Step 2 My money: Can I afford a portfolio career?

'Money feeds the stomach – and meaning and magic feed the spirit and the soul.' Mike Pegg (writer, consultant, presenter, mentor)

'How much do you need to earn?' This was the question Katie was asked when she first flirted with the idea of a portfolio career. Step 2 has an exercise to help you discover exactly this. There are several ways of funding a portfolio career start-up including: getting someone else to pay for you while you develop it; saving three to six months of money initially to see you through the set-up phase; working at a part-time job to 'pay the mortgage' while using the remaining time to create your portfolio; or the more risky, 'leap and the net will appear' approach.

Step 3 My motivated skills: Work I am good at, enjoy and am proud of

Bernard Haldane, an Englishman working in the US in the 1940s and onwards, was the first career development specialist to emphasise that we learn best from our successes rather than from our failures. He developed the notion of 'motivated skills.' A motivated skill is unlearned, genetic, linked to your temperament, something you are born with. It dictates how you prefer to behave.

Although there may be a finite number of motivated skills, they will only come together once in such a way that defines your uniqueness.

'You have a masterpiece inside you. One unlike any that has ever been created or ever will be. If you go to your grave without painting your masterpiece, it will not get painted. No one else can paint it. Only you.'
Gordon Mackenzie, *Orbiting the Giant Hairball*

Similarly, Oliver Wendell Holmes stated, 'Most of us go to the grave with our music still inside us'.

Whether through painting, music or the many other talents that may be dormant inside you, this Step has an activity that will help you to discover your motivated skills by analysing your key life achievements. You'll discover what drives you and motivates you to work – because unless you can find the opportunities to exercise these skills, you may experience boredom, frustration or even depression.

'It's about stretching your potential and being prepared to fail in pursuit of what you feel you should try to do.'
Carole Stone[27] (company director, social entrepreneur)

Step 4 My values: What makes me want to work?
Step 4 will help you to define your work values. You'll want to use your motivated skills but only in contexts that are consistent with what's important to you about work. Your values drive your journey through life and your motivated skills will determine how you behave on that journey. Each section of the book includes tips and tools to help with your travel plans.

'I'm a role model for my four-year-old son.' Chris Nel

'You have an in-tray at work but you have an in-tray in life too, which means you must prioritise what is important to you in life.'
Lisa Milnor

Step 5 My 'selves': Who do I want to be today?
Some psychologists suggest each of us has a number of 'selves' that co-exist – sometimes harmoniously, sometimes in competition – and that we switch between them. We decide what we're going to wear today. Similarly we decide, not usually consciously, what self we may project today. Having a career portfolio allows you to express something of the range of different 'selves' that you have. Step 5 explores this by using the Mr Benn stories as inspiration and invites you to become Mr Benn for a while 'as if by magic'. This Step will help to unveil the various selves that co-exist within you.

Step 6 My networks
This Step looks at using your networks to explore work options and how you can market yourself. You do this by:

- mining your existing networks;
- developing your support networks – finding the right people;
- connecting;
- growing your network by going to events or courses;
- growing via virtual networks;
- talking to people about your motivated skills and your achievements.

Step 7 My portfolio

Having networked, researched, explored and tried out all kinds of possibilities, you'll now have reached the stage of identifying possible jobs or careers for your portfolio. Step 7 will help you to draw up this list. This is still very much a testing-out phase where you'll try on different roles and different kinds of work 'for size'. You'll soon get a feel for the work you're doing and whether you're enjoying it.

You'll create relationships with almost everyone you meet and especially those you work for. Everyone has his or her own unique network. When you make a connection with someone else, they can choose to introduce you to their network of ideas or prospective customers. This is where you're likely to add the most value to your portfolio career. You learn quickly that you're the CEO of your own company.

Step 8 My story

This is very much your short personal story that will continue to develop every day. It's what you tell people when they ask 'and what do you do?' What are the first seven or so words that you say? How will that potentially benefit the person who's asking about you? How will you be memorable? Also, how will you describe yourself – and what you do – on any brochures, social networks and blogs? We help you to think through and refine the words so that you can tell your story in five, 15 and 60 seconds.

You'll be able to tell people about the 'benefits' of your portfolio not just the 'what'.

Step 9 My brand

'It's always show time.' David D'Alessandro, *Career Warfare*[28]

And don't you forget it...

Portfolio working requires a change of attitude – sometimes a big change. When asked what they do, many individuals reply, 'I work for the council' or 'I work for Microsoft', and a certain level of understanding and kudos is immediately acknowledged. With portfolio working, you have to convey quickly the 'what' *plus* the 'benefits' of what you do with confidence and clarity.

Welcome to your new digital CV

We suggest practical and innovative ways of marketing yourself. Setting up and getting the most out of your website, blog, Twitter, mobile phone, business cards, e-mail signature and learning to 'give it away'. We also discuss the benefits of self-marketing via word of mouth, public speaking and non-paid work.

'I talk rubbish.' Karen Cannard ('rubbish blogger', journalist, author, bead consultant, school governor)

'Getting you heard.' Katie Ledger

Step 10 My portfolio career: Next steps

This Step brings together all that you've learned about yourself and portfolio careers. How will you manage and develop your career? We invite you to project yourself into your future to explore who you'd like to be and the lifestyle you'd like to adopt. Many portfolio workers tell us they can't imagine working in any other way, while others may see it just as a temporary workstyle that may be attractive at one or more stages of their lives. Either way, there are changes of lifestyle to manage and in this section we introduce you to a model for understanding life changes and transitions. In addition, we examine the balancing act required when living a portfolio career within a portfolio lifestyle and the skills that will help you manage the pressures.

We look at how you can manage time and work effectively. One of the attractions for many is that, in theory, it should be more flexible for childcare, elderly care, disabled care, dual-career households, etc. There are real skills required to keep all these 'plates' spinning at the same time. And just how can you maintain those high energy levels essential to this workstyle?

We look at ways you can take something positive from mistakes and show how continuous learning, which is crucial for everyone, is the lifeblood for a portfolio worker. And we emphasise how it's particularly vital for portfolio workers to keep up with developments in new technologies.

The structure of this book

What follows are the 10 important Steps to focus on if you're to develop a profitable and fulfilling portfolio career. At the end of each Step, we provide a summary. Most of the Steps also have a variety of exercises or activities that we invite you to do to help your development. We call these 'CAN DOs' – because that is exactly what they are – things you *can do* to help you create a portfolio career.

We've interviewed 35 people for their stories which illustrate the issues around portfolio careers. You'll see many quotations from them. Most of our interviewees were happy to use their own names, but some preferred a *nom de plume*. We also quote widely from other people who've stimulated us with their observations and reflections.

One of the joys of the Web is it allows authors and readers to access and share the latest data, ideas, off-beat thoughts and research around the topic of portfolio careers. That's the idea behind our blog: **www. portfoliocareers.net**. We also encourage you to contact us with your thoughts and experiences. Today, it really is possible for writers to have ongoing dialogue with their readers who in turn become part of the creative process. You can contact us at:

barrie@portfoliocareers.net and **katie@portfoliocareers.net**

This book and our blog promote portfolio careers as a very real option today with many pluses for organisations, as well as for individuals. We've written this because we're excited about helping people to realise 'there is another way' to earn money, derive meaning and hey, even to sprinkle a little magic into our working lives.

And how do *we* answer the dreaded question, 'And what do you do?'

Simple. We say, 'I have a portfolio career'; then step back and wait for the questions that follow...

Barrie Hopson and Katie Ledger

Notes

1 Penelope's blog is **http://blog.penelopetrunk.com**. She's also written a book, *The Brazen Careerist* (Business Plus, 2007).
2 But according to **www.realage.com** he is only 53! Try this questionnaire for yourself.
3 **www.portfoliocareers.net**
4 Don Tapscott and Anthony Williams, *Wikinomics* (Atlantic, 2007).
5 *Classic Drucker* (Harvard Business School Press, 2006).
6 'Exploring the Future Workplace 2015+ and Tomorrow's People', CIPD Conference, 2007. Harrogate (UK).
7 **www.sliversoftime.com**
8 Baby boomers were born approximately from 1946–63; Generation X from 1964–80; Generation Y from 1981–95
9 Vodafone Working Nation Report 2008, Vol 2. Downloadable PDF from **www.workingnation.co.uk/index.php**
10 Michael Clinton, Peter Totterdell & Stephen Wood, 'A grounded theory of the portfolio working: experiencing the smallest of small businesses', *International Small Business Journal*, Vol 24, 2006, Sage Publications.
11 Office of National Statistics

12 Research into the Potential Take Up of Slivers-of-time working, Mel Evans, Lee Farenden-Smith, Danaa Nantogmah, Middlesex University, February, 2006

13 **www.startups.co.uk/6678842911504203557/working-five-to-nine.html**

14 2009 Women's Research: Untapped Potential: Stretching Toward the Future.

15 Random House, 2006.

16 On her blog she states 'Now I've found my niche as a career change coach and trainer, I help professionals in their 20s and 30s make fabulous career moves'. She does: so check her out at **http://freerangehumans.blogspot.com**.

17 'Tell it like it is', **www.talentsmoothie.com,** 2008

18 These results have been confirmed by an international in-depth survey of this age group by Don Tapscott in his book *Grown Up Digital: How the Net Generation Is Changing Your World* (McGraw-Hill, 2009).

19 'Age of Enlightenment', *The Guardian*, 6 May 2006

20 Research into the Potential Take Up of Slivers-of-time working, Mel Evans, Lee Farenden-Smith, Danaa Nantogmah, Middlesex University, February, 2006.

21 Reworking a Steve McDermott quotation from *How to Be a Complete and Utter Failure in Life, Work & Everything* (2nd ed, Pearson, 2007).

22 Although the research by Michael Clinton, et al (footnote 10), discovered that around half of their respondents found uncertainty to be a pleasant experience.

23 John Medina in *Brain Rules* (Pear Press, 2008) claims that in spite of the common use of the term all of the research suggests that we cannot multitask as such. He says that 'the best that you can say is that people who appear to be good at multitasking actually have good working memories, capable of paying attention to several inputs *one at a time*'.

24 **http://tinyurl.com/ckle5d**

25 'Working Life Begins at 50', learndirect/Careers Advice Service, 2008.

26 Cathleen Benko and Anne Weisberg, *Mass Career Customisation: Aligning the Workplace with Today's Nontraditional Workforce* (Harvard Business School Press, 2007).

27 Carole Stone, *Networking: The Art of Making Friends* (Vermilion, 2001).

28 *10 Rules for Building a Successful Personal Brand and Fighting to Keep It* (McGraw-Hill, 2004).

Step 1

My portfolio career: Is it for me?

Happy Hamster Wheel

'My life's my work and my work is my life and I love every minute of it.' Heather Jackson

---

A portfolio career can open up many paths for you. This assumes, of course, that you don't want to stay on the straight and narrow! Having more options keeps you viable and having a diverse portfolio of skills increases your value in the market. Managing your career as a portfolio allows you to take risks, remain flexible and – most importantly – to thrive in any economic situation. After every recession in the past

30 years, there has always been an immediate growth in self-employment.

Below is a questionnaire, a checklist, which should help you decide if a portfolio career is something you might like explore and to which you might be suited. We've isolated a set of characteristics by analysing our interviews with portfolio career workers. We've also drawn on the few academic studies carried out on people who've adopted this career pattern.

Questionnaire

For each statement below, ask yourself how strongly you agree with it. If you strongly agree, give yourself a score of '5'. If you strongly disagree, write in '1'. 2, 3, 4 are points in between.

1   I'm an excellent time manager. ___
2   I work well under pressure. ___
3   Financial security is less important than doing fulfilling work. ___
4   I'm not afraid to take risks. ___
5   I'm good at multi-tasking. ___
6   I get bored easily. ___
7   I manage stress well. ___
8   I love learning new things. ___
9   I learn from my mistakes. ___
10 I like working to deadlines. ___
11 I enjoy meeting new people. ___
12 I'm not a perfectionist. ___
13 I enjoy change. ___
14 I'm self-directed. ___
15 I believe that what happens to me is largely up to me. ___
16 I enjoy variety. ___
17 I have a high energy level. ___

18 I cope well with ambiguity. ____

19 I can improvise when not fully prepared. ____

20 I like being my own boss. ____

21 What happens in my career depends primarily on me. ____

22 I like being able to decide when and where I work. ____

23 I don't worry too much about the future. ____

24 There's little separation between my work and the rest of my life. ____

25 I can take tough decisions if necessary. ____

26 I enjoy revealing that I'm someone with many different sides to me. ____

27 I can be impulsive. ____

28 Overall, I feel good about myself. ____

29 I like new projects to work on. ____

30 People would describe me as assertive. ____

TOTAL ____

If your score is:

- Between 115 and 150, you should be a natural for a portfolio career.
- Between 65 and 114, you could have a portfolio career but you'll need to think and plan very carefully before taking the plunge.
- Between 30 and 64, you could find a portfolio career very demanding and stressful and might be better suited to a single-track, serial or lifestyle career.

Look at the questions on which you've scored less than three points. What is that telling you about yourself?

People who thrive on portfolio careers will strongly agree with the statements and share a number of general characteristics. They're likely to be self-starters, excellent time managers who organise their lives very well, believe they're largely in control of their own destiny, don't like to be bossed about, have a huge need for independence, are high energy, prepared to market themselves and actually enjoy connecting. They like change and variety, are not frightened to take risks, cope well with stress and pressure, feel positive about themselves, quite like having deadlines, love to learn, are not driven purely by money and are not over-anxious if they have insufficient funds at some times. They are also assertive, can multi-task, live with ambiguity and often blend their work and free time. The reason that perfectionists have problems with this career pattern is that there simply isn't the time to always get everything right.

On the downside people who have portfolio careers also talk about living permanently with smartphones or diaries in their hands. They can sometimes get fed up with constantly having to market themselves. There are often real financial risks to begin with and there may be greater pressure on immediate family for support. Holidays can be interesting:

'It's harder to do proper holidays. That doesn't really bother me. Because I'm happy in my working life, I need to holiday less. I'm celebrating each day. I always ask myself what was good about today? Mind you this approach isn't always popular with your family.' Richard Maude

Some people report feeling lonely as they're mainly working on their own. And of course you now have to find not one but a number of jobs to apply for and you have to find employers willing to hire you and who will accept your chosen workstyle.

Heather Jackson was very clear that you should only ever take on a job if it plays to your strengths. We have much more to say about that in Step 3.

We're not trying to put you off a portfolio career. We just want you to make a realistic choice as to whether this is right for you at this time in your life. As it happens, almost all of the people with whom we've spoken wouldn't choose another career pattern. Two of them returned to a single-track career at some point and reverted back to their portfolio careers within two months and four months respectively.

On the plus side we have Helen saying, 'Having this way of working makes me different and I like that.' And Lisa Milnor extolling the fact that, 'It's just me – I like that!'

Lisa also saw the huge plus of having the 'flexibility to live your life so you do what you believe in and feel passionate about. It also gives me time to do other things – like a triathlon and qualifying as an aerobics instructor – something I've wanted to do since I was 12.'

Katie said, 'Fifty per cent of my time I can dictate when I work. Very useful if you have two small children and a husband who also has a portfolio career. I also don't have some idiot manager who I don't respect telling me what to do.'

Betty Thayer, chief executive of **www.exec-appointments.com**, said: 'In the past people used to leave corporate life when they were ill. Now more and more of them are leaving to stay healthy. They want a better way of life and see the independent route as the way to achieve it.'

Steven D'Souza reflected that, 'When I was at school I always used to admire my peers who knew what they wanted to be when they were older. Some had chosen medicine, some law while others saw themselves as more creative and channelled their energy into sport or music. This certainty helped guide their choices in subjects, later their choice of degree and for many of them their current profession. I, on the other hand, knew what subjects I enjoyed, but the problem for me was that it was not one subject but many and I had far less certainty of what my career 'path' was. This led me at university to do a degree in theology and religious studies with history but also to undertake courses in Ancient Greek and Victimology! The benefit of having a wide range of interests is that I could see multiple points of view on subjects which those who had only studied with one lens were unable to distinguish. I think this intersectional insight is a blessing. The downside was that I never really specialised in just one thing, and some might say I had the curse of being a 'jack of all trades and master of none.'

Barrie said, 'I was always unemployable. Even when I was working at a university I got funding to set up a separate unit in the Psychology Department, as I didn't like the thought of having to report to someone who could force me to do things I didn't want to do. So I was able to recruit my own staff and if anyone in authority didn't like it, they knew the university would lose large sums of money. That gave me all the security I needed. I left eventually to set up my own company as I got bored with the politics. An example: they lost a £100k contract that I had negotiated because the committee to approve it was not going to meet for another month. That was the final straw.'

It's also interesting that many of our interviewees said it took between two and three years before they felt totally comfortable with their new workstyles. Most of this discomfort came from financial uncertainty.

A number of our interviewees have shared the experience of leaving or having to leave a big company. The contrast between working for a big brand organisation and finding yourself working from home, alone, with no financial security, no one running after you, or providing office support is huge. We encourage you to work through this book to really test out whether it's for you. In our experience, most people who have made the transition would never go back.

As an example, let's look at Katie's experience.

'I'd been working at ITN/Five News for eight years, as a news journalist and presenter. I'd taken redundancy once, had my second baby and come back part-time working for ITN News Channel, until that closed completely a year later. During that last year, I became disillusioned with the job. I no longer wanted to broadcast 'bad' news. I wanted to do something positive. I knew the News Channel was likely to fold and so looked at my options:

- get a journalist/presenter job elsewhere – more of the same – or
- retrain for another career or
- find a way to use all the skills, talents and experience I enjoyed using and see if I could help others to succeed.

I'd already been doing a few bits of work for individuals and companies, but couldn't see a way of making it into a full-time career. In the end, the News Channel closed nine months later and I made the bold decision to "leap", albeit with a bit of redundancy money still left in the bank.

I'd stayed connected with people I'd done a few projects for (i.e. technology geeks) and learned a new skill – how to use technology to my best advantage. This, over time, then helped me to network, create my story and brand.

I essentially missed out on the process which we describe in the first half of this book but with hindsight I would have found the Steps you are just about to read really useful.'

We were impressed by a guest posting on Hannah Morgan's blog, Career Sherpa: Guide for Lifetime Career Navigation[29]. The guest was Carol White Llewellyn. Does this ring any bells for you?

'I have often envied people who knew exactly what they wanted to do in life. My career path has been more like a canoe ride down an uncharted river. I ride the river until I see some interesting place to disembark, and I descend from my canoe to explore the territory. Sometimes on these excursions, I've stayed a matter of weeks or months (for temporary or consulting positions) and other times, I've

dwelled there many years when the rewards, learning and friendships were rich. I've always tried to give as much as, or more than, I've taken away. It's often difficult to get back in the canoe, especially when I've been happy where I was, and if I suspect the waters through which I must pass will be turbulent and the land ahead possibly less welcoming.

Yet I venture on, secure in the knowledge that each stop I've made has enriched me, that my canoe is full of tools and resources, knowledge and memories gathered along the way that further prepare me to handle whatever comes along. I am confident that what I've learned will greatly contribute to the people and places that welcome me into their midst in the future.

If you are in search of your next landing, take stock of the wealth of resources you have gathered in your canoe, even those collected in long-ago ports and distant lands. You never know which of your valuable assets will steer you to your next port o' call.'

So what do you think?

You've compared yourself against the characteristics that best describe successful portfolio workers. We've done our best to tell you about the downside. So, does it still sound a great idea? The next nine Steps walk you through setting up a portfolio career and we hope you'll enjoy yours as much as we love ours.

Summary
- You've assessed yourself against the characteristics of successful portfolio careerists.
- You've read about some of the problems that portfolio workers report facing.

- You've also heard about the reasons why they love this workstyle.
- So, is a portfolio career for you?

Notes
29 http://hannahmorgan.typepad.com/hannah_morgan/

Step 2

My money: Can I afford a portfolio career?

'Portfolio people lead cash-flow lives, not salary lives.'
Charles Handy[30]

What has led you into a portfolio career, or to consider a portfolio career?

Many of our interviewees were stimulated to do this following redundancy or unemployment. Others were returning to paid work after time out for raising their family. More said that they were just frustrated or bored with their current job. Some younger people, the Generation Ys who we talked with, were just starting out and were unable to decide on a single career. They wanted to experiment and explore. We spoke with women in their 30s and 40s who were managing a young family yet wanting paid work. Some people were approaching retirement and wanted more flexible working arrangements while at the same time wanting to learn something new. Others had already retired and wanted to get back into some paid work again but didn't want more of what they'd had before.

The reason for highlighting the differences in motivation is that your starting point will determine how you deal with the real issue of how you'll finance your portfolio career. If you've a 'significant other' who's got a 'secure' income, that can cushion the financial risk for a while. But if you don't have this, there are a few other ways to create your new career.

Four 'how to' strategies
1 **Get someone else to pay you while you develop it.**

We've been sent some very interesting suggestions from Marianne Cantwell[31], a career change coach, who specialises in helping Gen Ys develop their careers, including working towards a portfolio career.

- One good idea is to help with another business set-up. Working with a start-up in your industry allows you to gain exposure to a wide variety of experience, potentially getting involved in the marketing of the business, its development, as well as your usual role. This allows you to gain valuable experience that will benefit you when moving to your own creative mode of working. This, essentially, is learning with someone else's money.

- Another approach is to target the opposite to a start-up: namely working for a really, really big-name company. If you have a big, well-respected name under your belt, not only will you have fantastic contacts, but people will take you seriously when you take the plunge into a portfolio career.

- Most importantly, be brave enough to move around. Don't worry about the myth that people won't take you seriously unless you've been with a company for two years. Move after a year, 18 months – even six months – if you feel the role isn't helping your development.

- And don't just move to a similar position. Practise shifting the types of roles you do. This gives you more opportunity to sample what's out there and also to discover what you do like. In addition, it's great practice in re-branding and pitching yourself. If you get your single-track career right in your early 20s, by the time you're five years in you'll have a longer CV, more contacts, and wider experience than many people 10 or 15 years older than you.

- But what about those five years? Well you can still have a portfolio career in mind, even if you're working full time. Explore what you can do on the side. If you're working as a marketing professional, but envisage a cake-making business as part of your future portfolio, what is to stop you creating a small sideline making cakes for local fairs and weekend markets? You can build your reputation, get your product right, and have part of your portfolio developed for when you're ready to go it alone.

2 Save 3-6 months' money to see you thorough the set-up phase.

This is a strategy, which, on the face of it makes sense. And if you can do this, great. While it makes sense in theory, in reality, it may take you some time to achieve. How much money do you need to keep you afloat for six months? We tend to err on the side of caution and, while we applaud those that can actually do this, we feel it could be a good long-term excuse for not making the changes necessary. If on the other hand, you're lucky enough to get reasonable redundancy money, there's nothing stopping you. Apart from you, that is.

'Save three months' rainy day money and undergear your life – reduce your outgoings as much as possible.' Chris Nel

3 Work a part-time job to 'pay the mortgage' while using the remaining time to create your portfolio.

This is one that many portfolio careerists initially follow. Katie did this when she was a personal trainer. She wanted to work in TV as a reporter but didn't get paid anything to begin with. So she continued to do the personal training in the mornings and reported, edited, voiced and learned the skills required for TV in the afternoon. She also took on other jobs, such as voice-overs for educational books, reporting for in-flight movie programmes and acting, all of which was work that allowed her to expand the skills she had and enjoy the mix of roles. About a year later, she was able to drop her least exciting role, that of personal trainer, when she started getting paid to do a variety of TV related jobs.

So is there a job you could do to 'pay the mortgage', while building your ideal portfolio? Is there a job that's more than just money and could actually help build your network of contacts and opportunities? Is there a job that could be flexible enough so that if you got a 'portfolio' piece of work that needed to be done quickly, you could do it?

There are lots of permutations to this one, so have a think about how it's likely to work best for you.

'As long as you can earn enough to cover your mortgage and basic needs, be bold in other ways in trying to do what you really enjoy.'
Carole Stone

4 'Leap, and the net will appear' approach.

This can be attractive to some people. And it can work well. But we don't advocate this approach for everyone. It's really for those who feel OK with risk and happy to survive on very little. Generation Y-ers are well placed for this one because they generally don't have so many dependants, can choose to spend less and have more of a 'I don't care; I'm going for it' approach to life.

For those with dependants, it can be a risky approach. It may be that you've made enough great contacts to be reasonably certain that you'll have paying customers from day 1. But if you don't make enough money to get through your first three months, what are you going to do? What is your Plan B? Maybe it's back to the part-time job to 'pay the mortgage'.

Although we've said this is risky, there's another way to look at it. And that's by using the 'all or nothing' approach. Individuals who do this are really focused and motivated to attract work. They communicate widely, showcase their talents and follow people up. They make something happen. They get paid to do the kind of jobs they enjoy and play to their strengths.

Steven D'Souza[32] has these tips for those who are in employment and looking to create a portfolio career:

- Study something in your spare time that you're passionate about that will help you make a transition to your new career. I studied Organisational Consultancy at my own expense, which contributed greatly to helping me create value in education work.

- Think about starting what you want to do in the future now, even in a small way. For example, I wrote my first book while working full time. It took two years working in the evenings and at weekends but it got completed eventually and led to new opportunities. If you want to be a coach, start training clients for free to build your expertise until you're qualified to charge.

  Perform well in your current job and then look to negotiate a reduction in hours as you build up your new career, rather than give up your job all at once. This might mean doing four days a week or seeking another job that allows you to work more flexibly. Many companies are promoting flexible working practices and are open to requests if you're performing well in your role.

Of course, none of these approaches is absolutely rigid. You can use any combination but you do need to reflect on how you're now going to fund your new lifestyle. In our interviews, being made redundant appeared often as the spur to considering a portfolio career.

'When I was made redundant it didn't feel like liberation. It took three years before I began to feel comfortable and stopped worrying if the phone hadn't rung for a few days.' Richard Maude

'Risk' there clearly is and one of the characteristics that we highlighted in Step 1 was the ability to be able to live with financial uncertainty. Another portfolio career characteristic is that you will quite often work at different rates. Some jobs will pay well and others won't, but the lower-paying positions might be fun or offer intangible benefits, such as an opportunity to give back to your community.

You will almost certainly deal with a fluctuating income stream, which you can smooth by securing ongoing part-time contracts. Alone, these contracts might not be enough to live on, but when added to other contracts and jobs, they may well be.

Love your accountant

Not literally of course, unless your partner is one, which would be useful! If you don't already know a good accountant who can help you, find one. Ask your friends and other portfolio workers. Ideally, you need someone local and willing to teach you how to do basic finance, including accounts, invoices, VAT – if applicable, tax and any other mandatory activities. It can seem quite daunting to start with, but this is a skill you really should learn. There are many self-employed accountants and you'll probably find the person you're looking for via word of mouth. Ask the self-employed or small business people you know for recommendations. Also try local listings, newsletters and do a local search online. Many self-employed accountants don't want to work for large organisations and are happy to help local business people.

A good accountant can help you to:

- create a simple accounting system;
- manage your cash flow;
- work out your tax and VAT payments;
- tell you what to say to your local tax office.

You always need to know:

- how much is in your account;
- how much you are owed;
- how much you owe;
- whether you have enough money to pay your tax bill;
- whether you are registered for VAT;
- that you have enough to pay the bill. 'The taxman doesn't understand my work style. It can be a drain not knowing where your income is coming from. Three months ahead is as far as I can see.' Michelle Scally-Clarke (writer, performance poet, workshop designer and trainer, writer in residence, assistant director of the youth performing arts organisation, LS7 Results)

Wherever you're coming from, knowing something about your current expenditure is crucial. What are you spending now? Few people in our experience really give themselves enough time to analyse this. Yet, often these are the same people who will research minutely the cost of the latest smartphone, a pair of boots, an energy supplier or even the cost of butter.

How much you need to earn all depends on how much you want to spend. How much do you buy that you really don't need and use? Are you just stuck in the 'I want more and more' rut?

'Many people set aside their passions to pursue things they don't care about for the sake of financial security. The fact is, though, that the

job you took because it "pays the bills" could easily move offshore in the coming decade. If you've never learned to think creatively and to explore your true capacity, what will you do then?' Ken Robinson[33]

Daniel Pink adds to this line of thinking when, after analysing the future of jobs in the West, he clearly states that if someone overseas can do it cheaper and if computers can do it faster, those jobs will disappear. However, he's also saying that this frees us up to be creative, innovative and imaginative. Computers cannot (as yet) do this.[34]

Are you prepared to spend a little less to launch your brilliant new career?

CAN DO: What do I spend?

To start off, you need a budget spreadsheet. You can make up your own of course but we thought that you might find it helpful to see one that Barrie created for learndirect and is also contained in the book that he wrote with Mike Scally for the over 50s.[35] Go to http://tinyurl.com/mmpdt2 and log in. (This is free.) Go to the top status bar. Look for 'Money'. On the Money page, you'll see an exercise called Financial Health Check. Click that and follow the instructions to download it to your computer. Then save it somewhere safe and off you go.

Another example online that you might like to look at has been produced by Martin Lewis for his excellent money-saving site.[36] Both these sites will do all the adding up for you and will also show you, for example, just what percentage of income you spend in total on alcohol, or utilities or holidays. If necessary, you can change any of the headings so they better reflect your life. You can also insert or delete lines by right clicking any of the lines and choosing insert or delete.

A major barrier to us getting what we want out of life is the belief that: 'I can't afford to live on less than I earn or get now'. This activity will help you to record specific data on your outgoings and your income and then, crucially, invites you to assess just what you get from each of these expenditures.

WARNING: this piece of work does involve considerable preparation to be able to complete it accurately.

We suggest that you budget for a year. Look at:

- your bills for last year;
- direct debits;
- cheque books and bank statements;
- utilities bills;
- council tax charges;
- your rent/mortgage outgoings, and so on.

Work out the totals for the year for each heading. Divide by 12 and put that figure under each month. Estimate what you spend on other items: holidays, meals out, entertainment, travel, insurance, running your car and so on, then insert the average monthly spend. Most of us apparently underestimate what we spend on food and drink and also on clothes and going out. See what you find.

Now ask yourself these questions:

What does the picture tell you about your financial situation?

_____

_____

_____

What would you like to change?

_____

_____

_____

What might you need to change?

_____

_____

_____

What will it take to make the changes you want or need?

_____

_____

_____

CAN DO: What am I getting out of life for my money?

It's now time to see just what you're getting for the money you're spending. At the far right of your spreadsheet, add three columns, headed:

- essential
- nice to have
- can I spend less?

(If you're using **http://tinyurl.com/mmpdt2**, click on Financial Health Check again and you'll see that at the right-hand side of the table, the three columns with the headings are already there for you.) Consider each item on the spreadsheet and write/type in an X by each one you believe to be 'essential' to the way you want to live your life.

The next column asks you which of these items are 'nice to have'. Again, write/type in an X as appropriate.

With the third column – asking you if you could spend less on each item – write in scores as follows. Choose between giving the item a 1, which means absolutely not (i.e. you couldn't spend any less on it than you currently do); 2, which means 'to some extent'; 3, which says 'significantly' or 4, which says that you could 'drastically' reduce or even eliminate that expense.

If you're using the Martin Lewis spreadsheet, print it out, draw your columns to the side and follow the instructions given above.

Reflections

What occurs to you as a result of this activity?

_____

_____

_____

Are you surprised by anything that you've found?

_____

_____

_____

Which items could you cut down on or get rid of, if you chose to do so?

_____

_____

_____

The challenge for you will then be to convert some of these thoughts into objectives and to develop action plans to achieve them.

Many of us trap ourselves into a lifestyle because of assumptions we make of what we must have to make life worthwhile. Our 'hunger' can sometimes be so consuming that we pursue goals that aren't in our best interests and may not even be in line with our values. Step 4 will help you to define your work values so that you'll have a template against which you can measure your life and work decisions.

CAN DO: So how do I cut down on my spending?

The previous CAN DO should have helped you to identify some ways of cutting down on your spending, if you want to. We aren't advocating that everyone should cut back but it becomes important if the way you're currently investing your time and energy isn't giving you what you want.

Tips to save money

- Explore in store and then buy online.
- Always try to negotiate prices in smaller independent stores. It's now sometimes possible to do this in the larger chain stores.
- Ask for discounts for cash.
- Try home exchange schemes for holidays instead of renting.
- Shop at TK Maxx, Primark, discount shopping villages and wait for the sales.
- Buy second-hand copies of books from Amazon, Play or Abebooks.
- Pay off your credit cards. The interest rates can be horrendous.
- Use public transport instead of your car.
- Try using a carpool to get to work. Set one up if one doesn't exist.
- Shop around for insurance cover, utilities and telephone service providers. Use **www.uswitch.com** or **www.energyhelpline.com**.
- Sign up for Martin Lewis's 'Martin's Money Tips' at **www.moneysavingexpert.com**. Also buy his books second hand.
- Keep your car on the road for 10 years and run it into the ground.
- Use a pre-payment certificate to lower prescription costs.
- Drink tap water instead of that expensive bottled stuff.
- Check all invoices and receipts. Mistakes abound.
- Swap services with people you know, e.g. hairdressing for babysitting, cleaning for bookkeeping, etc.
- Avoid extended warranties.
- Bin the ready meals.
- Sell things on eBay.
- Ditch pay TV. Opt for Freeview.
- Send e-cards to people.
- Find what you want second hand through Freecycle at **www.uk.freecycle.org**.

- Book train journeys online and split the journey: Sheffield to Birmingham and then Birmingham to Reading instead of Sheffield to Reading. Savings can be enormous.
- Look at **www.petrolprices.com** for the latest prices close to your postcode.
- Use e-mail instead of letters.
- Get a recommendation for a specialist financial adviser.
- Read *Your Money or Your Life* (Penguin, 2008) by Joe Dominguez and Vicki Robin – on Amazon from 1p upwards if bought second-hand!

Highlight any of these that you currently do and then in a different colour highlight the ones that you are going to explore.

When are you going to start? Put a date by the side of the statement.

Which other tips could you give to us and to others? Write them down below.

_____

_____

_____

Do please e-mail them to us at **barrie@portfoliocareers.net** or katie@portfoliocareers.net

Getting financial support

It's always worth contacting Business Link (**www.businesslink.gov.uk** or look in your local phone directory). They should be able to point you in the direction of grants, business loans and local accountants. If you're thinking about setting up your own business and you're 50 or over, then you should contact PRIME in the same way (**www.primeinitiative.co.uk**). They offer workshops and have access to some limited funding.

Learning how to ask for money and managing your cash flow

Vaughan Evans in his book *Backing U*,[37] discusses just how difficult it can be for a small business person to insist that a customer pays up on time. 'You don't want to make too much fuss, because you want his custom again. Tough. You have no choice. You have to explain to your customer that whatever service you provide does not include acting as his banker.'

Ken Blanchard, Don Hutson and Ethan Willis remind us that 'making it in business requires three very important things – CASH, CASH, CASH'.[38] Most businesses that fail do so because of cash-flow problems not because of a lack of business.

So, one of the most crucial skills that you'll need to develop as a portfolio worker is asking for money and then negotiating a rate for the job. The general advice to people who are negotiating a salary for a new job is to leave money topics until after the job has been offered to you. By postponing this discussion you'll have enabled the employer to decide that they want you. Once they've made that decision, they'll be more reluctant to go back on it just because of money. Having said that, your first suggestion has to be roughly in the ballpark. So how do you know the parameters of the ballpark? This is where you use all of the networking skills that we describe in Step 6. Find people who are doing similar work and ask them what you should be charging. This is very different from asking them how much they earn. Use your social media sites. There are many sites for freelancers where you can contact people for advice on the going rate for a job (see Resources on page 231).

People who do freelance work as opposed to having a selection of actual jobs often ask us at what point do you introduce the topic of money or fees. Our advice is, as for a full-time job, leave it until the end. You'll very often find that contractors will themselves raise the issue. If they don't then you could say:

- 'Well, if you're happy with what we've discussed, we just need to address the money issue.'

or

- 'We've discussed everything very fully, so now we just need to discuss price.'

At this point, you do need to be clear about your daily rate. If it's a project, then you'll still need to think in terms of a multiple of your daily rate but you might well be prepared to discount that for a sizeable piece of work. You must be prepared to negotiate which means that you must have done your research. Barrie says that he always goes in at his highest daily rate: 'My usual daily rate is…'.

He says that you can tell immediately from the non-verbal reaction if this is in the right ballpark. This also establishes your credibility. You can always lower your rate if needs be because:

- 'This is a piece of work that I'd really like to do.'

or

- 'There are some new aspects to this work which means I'll learn from it, too.'

You must also have a price below which you aren't prepared to go *unless* there are other reasons for taking the job. You might genuinely see this as a useful learning experience, for example, or you might want to get this client onto your CV profile. Of course, you might just need to earn some money to keep you going in the short term. The danger with this is that you might find yourself anchored into a rate that's nowhere near what you believe you're worth.

After you've agreed an amount, put this in writing immediately and get a contract letter signed by the employer or contractor. This gives you legal protection and also enables you to double-check that you both share the same understanding of what you're going to be doing and what you'll get paid for doing it.

The other thing that you'll have to be prepared to do, especially if you're a freelancer, is to chase up your invoices. Remember first to send in your invoice immediately after the work is completed. You may be amazed to discover how many people don't do this. Remember the Blanchard quotation earlier. It's often very annoying to have to chase up payment as it takes time and can be a bit embarrassing. But don't be embarrassed. A contract has been agreed and you need to live. Quite often you'll find that there's been an oversight or the contractor just hasn't got round to processing your invoice.

For those of you still nervous about taking this step, it's worth listening to what Steve McDermott[39] had to say when he first went self-employed. He said that the most common response from his former colleagues was:

'"I couldn't handle the insecurity of being self-employed. Not knowing where my next pay cheque was coming from." At first I believed them, until I realised I had more security than them. No one could fire me, but me. And unlike their fixed salary, there was no limit to what I could earn. Sure, people thought I should be committed, and I was. Trouble is they meant to a secure unit for the insane.'

To put work and income into perspective, it's interesting to read the work of Marshall Sahlins, author of *Stone Age Economics*[40]. He discovered that historically, men appeared to hunt from two to two and a half days a week, with an average work week of 15 hours. Women gathered for about the same time. In fact, one day's work by a woman supplied her family with vegetables for the next three days. Throughout the year, both men and women worked for a couple of days, then took a couple of days off to rest and play games, gossip, engage in rituals and visit one another. The Industrial Revolution changed all of that. The paradigm shift that is now upon us is getting many people wondering if that prehistoric lifestyle may just have something attractive to offer but with all our modern conveniences. One pretty major downside was that most people didn't make it to 30.

Next steps

Review the information in this chapter.

Now write in what you want more of, less of and what you'd like to keep the same in your life right now.

	MORE OF	LESS OF	KEEP THE SAME
Things			
Income			

Pick the three that you would like to start working on right away.

Summary

- You've worked out how you'll fund your portfolio career.
- You've worked out how much you earn and how much you spend.
- You should be clearer on your total assets.
- You should also be getting some insights into what you're getting out of your life from the money you spend.
- You've learned how to get help with your finances.
- You've looked at how you negotiate rates for the job.

'We must walk consciously only part way toward our goal, and then leap in the dark to our success.' Henry Thoreau

www.portfoliocareers.net

Notes

30 *The Age of Unreason* (McGraw-Hill, 1990).

31 Marianne's website is **www.careerrevolution.co.uk** and her blog can be found at **www.freerangehumans.blogspot.com**

32 *Brilliant Networking: What the Best Networkers Know, Do and Say* (Pearson, 2008). See also **www.brilliantnetworking.net.**

33 *The Element: How Finding Your Passion Changes Everything* (Allen Lane, 2009).

34 *A Whole New Mind* (Marshall Cavendish, 2008).

35 Barrie Hopson & Mike Scally, *The Rainbow Years: The Pluses of Being 50+* (Middlesex University Press, 2008).

36 Go to Martin Lewis's site, **www.moneysavingexpert.com**, and find his budget_planner.xls.

37 *Backing U: A Business-Oriented Approach to Achieving Career Success* (Business & Careers Press, 2009).

38 *The One Minute Entrepreneur* (Headline, 2008).

39 *How to Be a Complete and Utter Failure in Life, Work and Everything* (2nd ed, Pearson, 2007).

40 *Stone Age Economics* (Aldine, 1972).

Step 3

My motivated skills: Work I am good at, enjoy and am proud of

I draw because I'm the luckiest man in the woRld.

(c)gapingvoid.com

'What a person is good at or not is a given. A person's way of performing can be slightly modified but it is unlikely to be completely changed – and certainly not easily.' Peter Drucker[41]

We all have things we love to do: making things, drawing them, designing them, inventing them, solving problems, writing, persuading, helping people, teaching, mentoring, networking...you get the idea.

We feel most alive when we do what we love to do and conversely we feel pretty miserable when we don't. Those 'things' are actually the skills that we were born to use – that we're 'motivated' to use. A motivated skill is unlearned, genetic; it's linked to our temperament and is something we're born with. It dictates how we prefer to behave.

Bernard Haldane was the first career development specialist to suggest we learn best from our successes and not our failures. He developed the concept of 'motivated skills' after moving to the US from England following the Second World War. Haldane worked with thousands of returning US service people and developed his approach from this experience. He was appalled at just how few people had any idea of what skills they had and what skills they wanted to use.

And he discovered that it was possible to identify at an early age what he was, by then, calling 'motivated skills'.

A four year old who enjoys performing will enjoy it at 15 or 20 or 80 – unless discouraged from doing so. A seven year old who's sensitive and likes to help people is also likely to want to do that throughout his or her life. Conversely, those who show no talent for constructing or building things early on are unlikely ever to love that activity, no matter how much training they receive. Someone who hates working with figures may laboriously acquire the skills to do so – but will never love it and won't look for opportunities to exercise that skill.

Dr Paul Samuelson, the first American to win the Nobel Prize in economics, put it succinctly: 'Never underestimate the vital importance of finding early in life the work that for you is play. This turns possible underachievers into happy warriors'.[42]

Although there is a finite number of motivated skills, only once will they come together in such a way that defines your uniqueness. Other writers use different words to describe this trait – strengths, signature strengths, dependable strengths, drivers, talents, etc. – but we'll stay with 'motivated skills' as it was the phrase Bernard Haldane used when he worked with Barrie in the 1980s.

There's a major publishing and consulting 'industry' that's developed over the past 10 years around helping people to develop their motivated skills or strengths.[43] The writers, researchers and consultants may not agree on what to call them but the one thing they all agree on is that people are wasting their time focusing on weaknesses and trying to fix them. How much easier and more logical to focus on motivated skills and get people to become even better at doing the things they love.

But sometimes we're actively discouraged from recognising our own skills as we 'might get above ourselves'. This is not just a peculiarity of the British but certainly there have been cultural pressures not to 'show off'. And there's certainly been strong cultural pressure to spend a great deal of time and effort in improving in the areas in which we are weak.

'Barrie shows no aptitude whatsoever for physics. This should be his major focus next year.' (From one of the author's recently rediscovered school reports. He still knows nothing about physics but this doesn't seem to have held him back that much!)

To quote Peter Drucker again, 'It takes far more energy and work to improve from incompetence to mediocrity than it takes to improve from first-rate performance to excellent.'

Grunt work and great work

There will always be things we have to do that we would prefer not to do. Mike Pegg calls this, 'grunt work'[44]. Any job we choose to do will have grunt work attached. The key is to ensure that it never takes up more than 20 per cent of your time. Sadly we all know people where that ratio is reversed.

Think of the job or jobs you currently hold. Name them and write down what you think is the 'grunt work' percentage and what you think is the work you love or 'great work' percentage.

Job 1 Title

percentage Grunt work _____ Great work _____

Job 2 Title

percentage Grunt work _____ Great work_____

Job 3 Title

percentage Grunt work _____ Great work _____

You'll only be doing work you love when you're using your motivated skills, so it's vital to find out what they are. That's what this chapter will help you to do. The challenge with having just one job is that it can be much more difficult to exercise all your motivated skills and to minimise your grunt work. If you can get some of it when you're working for one organisation and some of it elsewhere, then in theory everybody wins.

Michelle Scally-Clarke has five jobs (writer, performance poet, workshop designer and trainer, writer in residence, assistant director of the youth performing arts organisation LS7 Results). Clearly she's a portfolio worker, although she never uses the term. She captures beautifully what happens when you do the work you love.

'When I'm performing I'm understood. When I'm not performing I'm misunderstood. It's the biggest drug. You go to a different place. I'm an attention seeker and love saying in effect "look at me".'

She also stated from her experience in the US that when you're there 'you don't have to wear just one tag'.

People who're doing the work they love sometimes use phrases such as 'being in the zone' or 'going with the flow'. They report a level of total involvement in what they're are doing that renders time irrelevant. They're at one with what they're doing. It would be wonderful to feel that in all of the work that we do, but unrealistic: there will always be grunt work. The trick is to ensure that this represents only a small portion of our working time. Ken Robinson sums up this feeling very well:

'One of the strongest signs of being in the zone is the sense of freedom and of authenticity. When we are doing something that we love and are naturally good at, we are much more likely to feel centred in our true sense of self – to be who we feel we truly are. When we are in our Element, we feel we are doing what we are meant to be doing and being who we're meant to be.'[45]

Zulfi Hussain was very clear that no one job could ever satisfy all of his needs and enable him to use all of his skills. He has six jobs (as a BT employee, founder of Global Synergy Solutions, founder of Global Promise, and non-executive director of three companies):

'I love the unusual combination of activities'. He also had the interesting comment, 'in South East Asia, people generally do more than one job. In eastern philosophy the skills are in the person not in the work. In the UK, one in 10 Asians start up at least one business in their lifetime but the ratio is one in 100 for indigenous whites.'

Helen has five jobs (adviser/consultant to a school, supply teacher, supporting students on PGCE course, regional subject adviser, exam marker) and says that she can mentally separate out all of the jobs in terms of the skills she likes to use.

Veronique Jaquard, who has four jobs (restaurant *maître d'*, shopkeeper, bookkeeper and administrator for family business, patisserie chef), says:

'Full-time jobs can be boring. I love the change of routine. You get so many more opportunities to develop than if you have one job.'

Katie says that she didn't know what her skills were until she started to 'sell' herself. Well, that can be a painful and drawn-out way of discovering your motivated skills so we've devised an easier and quicker way of doing this, based upon the approach that Bernard Haldane taught Barrie.

CAN DO: List your achievements

An achievement must satisfy three criteria:

1 you believe you did it well;
2 you enjoyed it;
3 you felt proud of it.

This isn't easy for many of us. Generally we're not taught to think about what we've achieved and some of us still have problems in defining what we're good at, what we're proud of and what we enjoy. It's now time to shake off those shackles of humility and modesty. Each one of us has achieved much and those achievements are unique to us. We may not have generated world peace or a cure for AIDS, but we all will have a variety of things in our lives about which we should feel proud.

'It feels weird looking at and talking about achievements – but there was massive value in going through the cringe factor.' Tim[46]

'You almost have to use a different part of your brain in order to consider your achievements as it is an alien concept.' Alison

Again, all too often, we *think* we've achieved something only to be told that it's not that great. Barrie is not known for his practical skills. At the age of 12, he was very proud of creating a wooden letter rack with a fretwork design cut out at the front. After three months' toil, he delivered it to the woodwork teacher. It was placed on the table at the front of the class and the teacher laughingly asked the class if they'd seen anything more pathetic. 'What a waste of three months. Anyway, your mother might like it.' Actually his mother did like it and Barrie found it in her possessions after her death 50 years later. Not surprisingly, he never attempted to make anything else, but wrote books instead.

Research has demonstrated that the simple act of recalling and talking about our achievements helps us to feel more positive. This may not be very surprising but it's interesting to note how infrequently people actually do this simple exercise when the potential benefits are so great. The process also appears to set them on a path, 'to propel themselves forward with energy and direction towards a future that they would be proud to create'.[47]

Here's a simple exercise. On a sheet of paper, write down what you think your biggest achievement is in your life so far. Also put down how old you were at the time. Now think of all of your other achievements. Go back to when you were under 10. Barrie's was manoeuvring to play the part of Joseph in the school nativity play at nine, so that he could get close to the girl he fancied who had the part of Mary. Katie still remembers with pride when, aged seven, she won the school Easter card competition with a winning collage of ribbon and hundreds and thousands.

Think back to your teenage years, your time at school, further education or training. Picture yourself in your first job, then all of the other jobs you've had.

- What were you doing outside your paid work?
- Did you achieve at hobbies, social activities, unpaid work and leisure pursuits?
- What were your achievements within your family and friends networks?
- What did you learn to do?
- Did you help others?

- Did you teach others?
- Did you manage or organise or lead others?
- Did you make or create something?
- Did you travel somewhere?
- Did you persuade someone about something?
- Did you communicate really well at some point?
- Did you perform?
- Did you research something really well?
- Did you persist with a plan until you actually got what you wanted?
- Remember to put the age you were at the time next to each achievement.

By now, you should have filled up quite a lot of that sheet of paper. If not, ask some friends, a partner, parents or other family members. Explain that you're doing this to discover what you're really good at. You could offer to do the same for them at a later date.

CAN DO: Rank order your achievements

Look at your list and tick off the seven achievements of which you are most proud, you did well and you enjoyed the most. Write them below starting with what you consider to be your No.1 achievement.

1 _____
2 _____
3 _____
4 _____
5 _____
6 _____
7 _____

You can always add some additional achievements if you feel that seven is not enough.

CAN DO: What are the most common motivated skills?

Below is a table of 27 of the most commonly recalled motivated skills plus three blank areas. These are for you to write in any skills that you've used to gain your achievements and that we haven't listed.

MY MOTIVATED SKILL IS:	MY MOTIVATED SKILL IS:	MY MOTIVATED SKILL IS:
Giving credit to others Recognising and appreciating the achievements of others.	**Sensitivity** Understanding the feelings of others and being able to make people feel comfortable, intuitive.	**Managing time** Setting priorities, making lists, working to schedules, keeping to appointments.
Being innovative Creating, innovating, seeing alternatives, developing new ideas.	**Teaching** Teaching, training, coaching, mentoring.	**Analysing** Managing and organising information, examining, dissecting, sorting through.
Reviewing Being able to stand back and learn from an experience.	**Working creatively** With ideas, spaces, shapes, events, faces; thinking laterally.	**Selling** Persuading, influencing, negotiating, promoting change.
Solving problems Diagnosing, researching, assessing pros and cons.	**Motivating and leading** Inspiring and energising others to achieve.	**Adaptability** Flexible, expecting and welcoming change, able to live with ambiguity.

Organising people Managing and organising people to get tasks done.	**Strategic thinking** Being able to stand back, seeing the big picture, construct the pictures of the future.	**Performing** In a group, on stage, one to one, using showmanship.
Helping others Committed to and good at doing things and providing good service to others.	**Managing money** Organising finances, budgeting, keeping records.	**Improvising** Adapting, experimenting, trial and error.
Practical Making things, constructing things, mending them.	**Using technology** Word processing, spreadsheets, internet, PDAs, etc.	**Being curious** Having an enquiring mind, keen to pursue new knowledge, questioning.
Physical activities Sports, travelling, outdoor activities.	**Networking** Knowing how to make contacts and to market oneself and others.	**Assertiveness** Telling people what you want or prefer, clearly and confidently without threats or putting yourself down.
Having high energy Being able to take on lots of projects, rarely tired.	**Persistence** Doesn't give up easily, hangs on in there.	**Communicating** With words, written, spoken, face to face, in groups, blogging, etc.

Now look at the table on the next page. You will see along the top the references to each of your seven achievements.

Write the name of each one in the top line.

You should now look down the Motivated Skills column and ask yourself: 'Did I use this skill to help me to get my No. 1 achievement?'

Use your imagination. Take yourself back to the age and the time when you created that achievement. Ask yourself: 'What did I do to make that happen?'

Never ask yourself 'why?'

Do this for all of your achievements. This activity will enable you to look at the greatest achievements in your life to date so that you can discover which motivated skills you use most often. Tick each skill that you recall using which helped you to reach that achievement.

MY ACHIEVEMENTS

Motivated skills	1	2	3
Solving problems			
Motivating and leading			
Adaptability			
Reviewing			
Working creatively			
Selling			
Giving credit to others			
Sensitivity			
Managing time			
Being innovative			
Teaching			
Analysing			
Organising people			
Strategic thinking			
Performing			
Helping others			
Managing money			
Improvising			

4	5	6	7	Totals

MY ACHIEVEMENTS (continued)

Motivated skills	1	2	3
Being practical			
Using technology			
Being curious			
Physical activities			
Networking			
Assertiveness			
Having high energy			
Persistence			
Communicating			
TOTAL			

Count up the number of ticks that you have in each row and put the total into the end 'Totals' column.

Which are the six or seven skills that you used the most? Write them below:

1 _____

2 _____

3 _____

4 _____

5 _____

6 _____

7 _____

4	5	6	7	Totals

These represent the skills that, when you use them, make you feel good, fulfilled and alive. These are the skills you're motivated to use. Success for you will result from using these skills. Don't waste your time trying to develop skills that don't produce this effect. So many people spend time attempting to compensate for their weaknesses when they should be getting even better at using their motivated skills.

'Knowledge of which skills are motivated gives you a handle on how to use them, develop them, train and educate them, combine them in different ways to meet changing job and educational demands.'
Bernard Haldane[48]

David Marriott, a financial analyst, found it challenging to talk about himself at interviews. He was taught this technique of identifying and analysing his achievements. He went for an interview at Harley Davidson.

'You have to change your mindset. You have to really think what an achievement is. I don't usually think that way. I remember one incident when I was a lifeguard. My role was to co-ordinate all the rescue services including the helicopters. I stayed calm and was able to make sure everyone was where they were supposed to be. We saved a man's life.

Listing my motivated skills was quite difficult at first but then thinking about broadening them out – not just work achievements – made it easier. Motivated Skills (MS) helped me to talk about myself, particularly at job interviews. I have a level of shyness and it meant I could describe me as if I was selling someone else. It turned out I was selling me! I had the 'proofs' (I could articulate the evidence) of my skills. I was prepared.

MS was very useful in that it helped me to clarify what I felt good at doing and why. Also, importantly, it helped me articulate it. By the way, I had the interview on Tuesday and they offered me the job on Friday'.

CAN DO: How many of your motivated skills are you using now?

One of the pluses of a portfolio career is that you're maximising your chances of employing a greater percentage of your motivated skills. But remember the comment from Penelope Trunk on page 1:

'A portfolio career is not the same thing as holding down three bad jobs and wishing you could figure out what to do with yourself. Rather, it is a scheme you pursue purposefully and positively, as a way to achieve financial or personal goals or a mixture of both.'

Now is the opportunity to find out just how many of your motivated skills you're using at this moment in your life. In the table below write in your top six or seven motivated skills in order of importance to you (your previous rankings) and ask yourself how far that skill is used in your existing job if you have only one. If you have more than one, ask the same question for that. Next, see if you can visualise a job or jobs that you think you might enjoy. Name them all in the top row and then ask yourself the question:

'How much opportunity does this job give me for using this motivated skill?'

If your present job allows you to fully utilise that skill, award it a 10. If it doesn't allow you to use it all, award it a 0. Or award it points in between as best you can.

Do the same for any jobs you might be considering. You'll see that the table gives a weighting for your scores. So, for example, if teaching was your No. 1 motivated skill that would appear first and you would rate that. If you had a reasonable opportunity to use that skill, you might give it an 8. In the table that would be multiplied by 7 so would give you a score of 56.

Do this for each of your motivated skills for each job until you have totals for each one.

MY JOB/S AND MY MOTIVATED SKILLS

My motivated skills	JOB 1	JOB 2	JOB 3	JOB 4	JOB 5
Skill 1	_x 7 =	_x 7 =	_x 7 =	_x 7 =	_x 7 =
Skill 2	_x 6 =	_x 6 =	_x 6 =	_x 6 =	_x 6 =
Skill 3	_x 5 =	_x 5 =	_x 5 =	_x 5 =	_x 5 =
Skill 4	_x 4 =	_x 4 =	_x 4 =	_x 4 =	_x 4 =
Skill 5	_x 3 =	_x 3 =	_x 3 =	_x 3 =	_x 3 =
Skill 6	_x 2 =	_x 2 =	_x 2 =	_x 2 =	_x 2 =
Skill 7	_x 1 =	_x 1 =	_x 1 =	_x 1 =	_x 1 =
Total					

If you gave 10 points for each of your 7 motivated skills your maximum total would be 280, although it's highly unlikely that anyone would achieve that score.

Now answer the following questions for yourself:

1 How much opportunity is there overall in your current job for you to use your motivated skills?

_____

_____

_____

_____

2 Do any of the other jobs that you've considered fit your motivated skills more closely?

_____

_____

_____

_____

3 How do the jobs compare in the scoring?

_____

_____

_____

4 Does this feel right? If not, why not? Remember that intuition is just as important as numbers – probably more so.

_____

_____

_____

5 Do your answers suggest questions that you might wish to ask at a job interview?

_____

_____

_____

_____

'My full-time job gave me little opportunity to play to my strengths so I left it at the same time that I was going through a divorce with two small children. But I knew what my strengths were and I liked myself. At 33, that's a massive strength. So I walked into the CEO's office of a large bank in Yorkshire and 'tried out an idea on him' and said this is what it could do for the bank and other similarly large organisations and that I wanted to set up and go it alone.

He completely supported the concept and the delivery. I can't emphasise enough how important that first voice of approval is to you...the confidence it brings, gives you the attitude you can take on the world, your idea is not stupid and ill conceived, it can actually work, and the only person stopping you from delivering itis yourself, that is a wonderful feeling. The next day I went to my accountant who also believed in me and he said that I needed a name for my company so the thread that had run through these conversations was these people believed in me and so did I. Hence my company was named Believe Corporate Relations, and from that day on I've never looked back.' Heather Jackson (Managing Director of Believe Corporate Relations, strategic business and marketing consultancy)

'We don't know who we can be until we know what we can do.' Ken Robinson[49]

Summary

- Play to the skills you're motivated to use. Forget the ones you don't enjoy.
- We all have a unique set of motivated skills we're born with and want to use.
- When we use our motivated skills, we feel alive, energised and fulfilled.
- You'll have identified at least seven of your greatest achievements. This is something you enjoyed, were proud of and did well.
- You've identified your key motivated skills.
- You've assessed all the jobs that you currently do or are thinking about to see which ones rank highest in terms of fulfilling your motivated skills.

Remember what George Eliot said, 'It's never too late to be what you might have been'.

'Successful careers develop when people are prepared for opportunities because they know their strengths, their method of work and their values. Knowing where one belongs can transform an ordinary person – hardworking but otherwise mediocre – into an outstanding performer.' Peter Drucker[50]

Notes

41 Peter Drucker, *Managing Oneself* (Harvard Business Review Publishing, 2008).
42 'How I became an Economist', **www.nobelprize.org/nobel_prizes/economics/articles/samuelson-2/index.html**
43 This includes writers and presenters such as Mike Pegg, Marcus Buckingham, Tom Rath, Martin Seligman and Donald Clifton.
44 Look at Mike Pegg's blog periodically to keep up with his thinking and developments relating to strengths: **www.strengthsacademy.com**
45 Ken Robinson, *The Element: How Finding Your Passion Changes Everything* (Allen Lane, 2009).
46 David Pilbeam, unpublished MA thesis, 'How can coaching help people discover the patterns of their achievements and aid career development?', Oxford Brookes University, 2008.
47 D P McAdams, *The Stories We Live By: Personal Myths and the Making of the Self* (The Guildford Press, 1993).
48 *Job Power Now: the Young People's Job Finding Guide* (Acropolis Press, 1976).
49 *The Element: How Finding Your Passion Changes Everything* (Allen Lane, 2009).
50 *Managing Oneself* (Harvard Business Review Publishing, 2008).

Step 4

My values: What makes me want to work?

"Cheshire Puss, asked Alice, would you tell me, please, which way I ought to go from here? That depends a good deal on where you want to go, said the Cat. I don't much care where, said Alice. Then it doesn't matter which way you go, said the Cat." Lewis Carroll, *Alice's Adventures in Wonderland*

From time to time, we need to ask ourselves questions about our values, about what's important to us, such as:

- How do I like to spend my time?
- What kind of people do I choose to have around me?
- Where do I want to live and to work?
- How important to me are money, status, independence, creativity, making decisions, taking risks, helping others, security, success and so on?

Being able to answer questions like these is crucial to helping us choose the kind of work that we want to do. The more we're able to live our values in our work, the more rewarding our careers will be.

As we grow up, we absorb 'messages' and influences from our parents, our families, our teachers, our friends and ultimately from the media and the culture we engage with. We emerge as adults with our own selection of beliefs, preferences and priorities about what matters to us, what's most important for us to do, to be, to have, to aspire to and to work for. Each of us has a unique combination of values that influences and shapes our decisions and behaviour.

Values affect how we judge and assess our life and the experiences it presents us with. For example, if we value independence, we won't be happy if faced with a job in which we're closely supervised. If we prize challenge and adventure, we're unlikely to survive in routine or bureaucratic work. Following a career that's aligned with our values is much more likely to result in high levels of satisfaction, motivation, commitment, health and well-being. We may be highly competent in a particular area, but if what we're doing is out of line with our values, it might well be problematic for us.

Our values become apparent early on in life and are more stable than attitudes and interests. It's these values that drive us and motivate us to do and not to do certain things and to make choices every day.

CAN DO: What are my work values?

Here's an opportunity for you to identify your key work values[51]. This exercise will:

- invite you to reflect on key work values and decide how they apply to you.
- ask you to identify up to eight work values that are most important to you and see how far your work currently measures up to them.
- ask you to identify values that may not be included here but that you know influence your decisions and your work choices.

Appendix 1 consists of 40 value cards, which you need to cut out. There are 32 work value cards and also five with the following headings

Very important
Important
Quite important
Of some importance
Not important

In addition to the 32 value cards and the five header cards, you'll also find three blank cards.If you think that some of your values are missing from the printed cards, then please write them in on these.

Place the five heading cards in front of you from left to right and from most to least important, as indicated:

Very Important Important Quite Important Of some Importance Not Important

Look at each of the 32 work value cards in turn and ask yourself the question: **How important is this for me in paid work?**

- Working through the cards in turn, place each under the 'importance' category heading which best describes how important that value is to you.
- After sorting the cards into the five categories, make certain that there are no more than eight in the 'very important' one. If there are, look at the cards again to refine further your values. At the same time, do ensure you have at least four or five under 'very important'.
- When you've finished grouping all the value cards, look at each category in turn. Then arrange the cards under each category heading, ranking them from the most to the least important.

- Now write them in the table below in rank order.

MY VERY IMPORTANT WORK VALUES
1
2
3
4
5
6
7
8
MY NOT IMPORTANT VALUES
1
2
3
4
5
6
7
8

- Next, write down the name of your current job, assuming you have one. You'll know your current job well and have some idea whether it reflects your work values. This activity will help you to discover to what extent this is so, or whether you might be better off considering alternative jobs or indeed additional jobs, if you're contemplating a portfolio career. If you already have more than two jobs, add them to the table below. If you do not have a job at the moment then focus on options that you want to consider.

- Write in the values that you've identified as 'very important' and those that you've said are 'not important' to you at all.
- How far does your present job satisfy this work value?
  If that value is never satisfied by your job, award it 0 points.
  If that value is totally satisfied, award it 10 points.
  Please use the full range from 0–10.
  You'll see that a weighting of your answers has already been filled in for you. Simply complete the calculations. For example:

  $6 \times 8 = 48$
  $8 \times 7 = 56$
  $2 \times 6 = 12$ etc.

- Now do the same for any other jobs you might be considering.
- Add up the totals for each job you've analysed.

If you gave 10 points for each of your eight 'very important' life values, your maximum total would be 360, although it's highly unlikely that anyone would achieve this score.

MY JOB AND MY VALUES

VERY IMPORTANT	MY CURRENT JOB	JOB / OPTION 2	JOB / OPTION 3	JOB / OPTION 4	JOB / OPTION 5
1		__ x 8 =	__ x 8 =	__ x 8 =	
2		__ x 7 =	__ x 7 =	__ x 7 =	
3		__ x 6 =	__ x 6 =	__ x 6 =	
4		__ x 5 =	__ x 5 =	__ x 5 =	
5		__ x 4 =	__ x 4 =	__ x 4 =	
6		__ x 3 =	__ x 3 =	__ x 3 =	
7		__ x 2 =	__ x 2 =	__ x 2 =	
8		__ x 1 =	__ x 1 =	__ x 1 =	
TOTAL					

MY NOT IMPORTANT CARDS ARE:

Tick any of these if they feature in your current job or any alternative jobs

1					
2					
3					
4					
5					
6					
7					
8					

This also asks for your 'not important' values. These are useful so that later you can assess how much doing things that you don't value might crop up in your job.

With your list of key work values you now have a tool that you can use to analyse the suitability of any key work decision – about choosing or accepting a job, how the jobs in your current portfolio rate and how jobs that you are considering stand up.

Now answer the following questions for yourself:

1 How much opportunity is there overall in my current job for me to express my work values?

_____

_____

_____

2 Do any of the values in my 'not important' list feature in my present job?

_____

_____

_____

3 Do any of the other jobs that I've analysed more closely fit my key values?

_____

_____

_____

4 How do the jobs compare in the scoring?

_____

_____

_____

5 Does this feel right? If not, why not?

_____

_____

_____

6 Do you need additional information before making a choice?

_____

_____

_____

7 Do your answers suggest questions that you might wish to ask at a job interview?

_____

_____

_____

8 Can you think of any objectives that you might want to set yourself as a result of this activity?

_____

_____

_____

Changes in work and life values

There would appear to be a significant and global shift in values. Ronald Inglehart[52] and his colleagues from the University of Michigan have been tracking and comparing public opinion across many countries for the past quarter of a century. His World Values Survey, which covers 85 per cent of the world's population, has, year on year, noted greater concern for spiritual and non-material matters. He's identified that both life satisfaction and happiness have increased across the majority of the nations. Having greater choice and a feeling of control seems to be crucial to increased well-being as muchas economic growth and democratisation.

Daniel Pink[53] talks of 'meaning being the new money'. Victor Frankl, 50 years ago, noted that, 'People have enough to live, but nothing to live for; they have the means but no meaning'.

Portfolio workers consistently tell us that a major driver for their choice of career pattern is being able to create a work style that provides them with meaning. What do your scores suggest about what your work values are saying to you as to what is important in your working life?

Peter Drucker[54], as always, has something significant to say about the importance of living by your values. He constructed what he liked to call 'the mirror test'. He recalls an incident in 1906 when the highly respected German Ambassador in London abruptly resigned rather than preside over a dinner given by the diplomatic corps for Edward VII. The king was a notorious womaniser and made it clear what kind of dinner he wanted. The ambassador is reported to have said, 'I refuse to see a pimp in the mirror in the morning when I shave'. This is the mirror test. Ask yourself: 'What kind of person do I want to see in the mirror in the morning?'

Remember the wonderful lines from comedian Demetri Martin, 'I ordered a wake-up call the other day. The phone rang and a woman's voice said, "What the hell are you doing with your life?"'

Summary

- You've identified what is and what is not important to you about work.
- You've uncovered up to eight values that you need to find in the work you do.
- You'll have found out how your existing job or jobs measure up.
- You can see how alternative jobs might compare.
- Because your values are relatively stable, you can rate any job in the future.

Notes

51 This is adapted from the *Life Values Activity* in *The Rainbow Years: The Pluses of Being 50+* by Barrie Hopson and Mike Scally (Middlesex University Press, 2008).
52 R. Inglehart, R. Foa, C. Peterson & C. Weizel, 'Development, freedom and rising happiness: A global perspective', Perspectives on Psychological Sciences, 3, pp. 186–189, 2008.
53 *A Whole New Mind* (Marshall Cavendish, 2008).
54 *Managing Oneself* (Harvard Business School Press, 2008).

Step 5

My 'selves': Who am I going to be today?

As if by magic – Mr Benn

The very British Mr Benn[55] was a well-loved character in children's books with

an accompanying TV series during the 1970s. He was a respectable-looking character, replete with business suit and bowler hat, living at 52 Festive Road in a London suburb. What made him different and special was that he used to visit a fancy-dress shop where he was invited by the moustachioed, fez-wearing shopkeeper to try on a particular outfit. From the back of the changing room he would leave the shop through a magic door and, 'as if by magic', enter a world appropriate to his costume, where he had an adventure (which usually contained a moral) before the shopkeeper re-appeared and the story ended.

Mr Benn then returned to his normal life as a businessman but was left with a small souvenir of his magical adventure.

The parallel for us is that most of us refer to ourselves as if there was just one of us: one self. But actually each of us has a number of selves that we switch between. We wake up in the morning and decide what we are going to wear today. Similarly, we will decide, not usually consciously, what 'self' we will wear today. The difference between the two being that we will usually not have too many changes of clothes but during the course of a day we may go through the 'magic door' many times and try on a number of selves. Like Mr Benn, we will have different experiences and adventures with our different selves and like him we will return from each with a small souvenir which will stay with us forever.

Psychologists for years have advocated the importance of finding our 'true self'. In a book on reinventing your career, Herminia Ibarra[56] says that:

'We must...abandon the conventional career advice queries – 'Who am I ?' – in favour of more open-ended alternatives – 'Among the many possible selves that I might become, which is the most intriguing to me now?'

Two Stanford cognitive psychologists[57] discussing this multi-self model claimed that we all carry around in our hearts and minds a whole cast of characters, the selves we think we are and those that we would like to become or even that we might fear becoming in the future. In other words, like Mr Benn, we are continuously trying on new outfits for size, returning to the ones with which we are familiar and speculating about who next we might wish to be.

What is also interesting is that sometimes your posture and movement, voice and vocabulary might be different as you play each role. Yet these roles are not external to you; they are who you are.

You will see immediately that one huge plus of a portfolio career is that it's ideally suited to the notion of multiple selves. Within a single-track career it'll certainly be possible to try out some different selves but a portfolio career will offer significantly more opportunities.

CAN DO: As if by magic

This is a good exercise to do with a friend or colleague if possible, but in the instructions below we'll assume that you're doing it on your own.

Imagine you're Mr Benn. You're going into the magic shop and the shopkeeper says to you, 'Good morning, and who would you like to be today?'

To help you to answer this, think back to yesterday. Who were you yesterday? How many of you were there? Don't just think about work, think of your life in total. For example, Katie interviewed Barrie about what roles he played yesterday. This was his answer:

'I was a grandfather; I was a networker; I helped someone over the phone with a career issue; I was a good friend; I was a *bon viveur* – enjoying good food and wine; I was a writer; I was a mentor; I was an absentee husband; I was a helpful parent; I was a learner – learning to use a Mac instead of a PC; I was a very organised person – sorting out the debris in my home office; I had some telephone calls in my role as a Chairman of a small IT company; I was a sales person – persuading someone to buy my time to present a masterclass; I shredded a great deal of paper which I will mix in to my compost heap; I fantasised about how I would love to have been a professional cricketer as I watched a 20/20 match on TV; I thought about being a volunteer foster owner for stray cats.'

Note that he was telling Katie about things that he felt good about, some things he did not feel quite so good about, and some things that he fantasised about. He was telling her in effect that he had a series of selves:

- Chairman of an IT company;
- writer;
- sales person;
- professional cricketer;
- friendly *bon viveur* who enjoys life and his friends;
- parent and grandparent;
- someone who works at saving the planet;
- cat fosterer;
- mentor;
- someone who enjoys learning new things;
- someone who could be a better husband.

This was just from one day. Barrie was then asked to think of other selves that might have emerged out of that Magic Door but that are not part of his present life. He proffered the following:

- an entrepreneur constantly coming up with new ideas for exciting and financially rewarding businesses;
- volunteering to work in Africa to help communities to develop themselves into entrepreneurs;
- a novelist;
- a journalist with a regular column;
- an excellent chef;
- a creator of fun and exciting social events.

You get the drift. He could have had a whole series of Mr Benn episodes all to himself! So you have a go. What were the different selves that came into your day yesterday? Write them in the space provided opposite.

1 _____
2 _____
3 _____
4 _____
5 _____
6 _____
7 _____
8 _____
9 _____
10 _____

Now think back over your life. If you have already completed the Life Achievements CAN DO (on page 68), then you might want to remind yourself of your answers. How many additional different selves emerge from this recollection?

1 _____
2 _____
3 _____
4 _____
5 _____
6 _____
7 _____
8 _____
9 _____
10 _____

You now have a list of all of the different lives you're living, could live or have lived by looking at what you do now and what you might like to do. Rank them in order of what you would define as your top five selves and write them below:

1 _____

2 _____

3 _____

4 _____

5 _____

Now look at the possible job components that you have or are considering for your career portfolio. List them below left. Then ask yourself for each of these which of your selves can be expressed in each job (there may well be more than one for each).

My possible jobs	Which of my selves would this satisfy?
1	
2	
3	
4	
5	

What will emerge from this is just how many of your different selves you'll be able to live out by having more than one job. Portfolio workers may not actually 'have it all' but they're a good way down the road – especially when compared with their single-track career contemporaries.

The artwork opposite produced by Silje Alberthe Kamille Friis, from Denmark, depicts the concept beautifully.

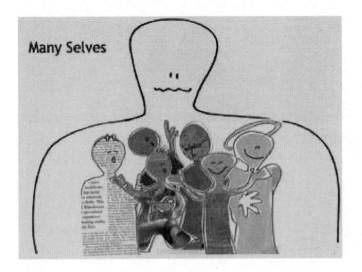

Many Selves

Summary
- We all have a variety of different selves within us.
- You've identified which selves make up your behavioural repertoire.
- You've examined each of the jobs that you do or are hoping to do and researched which of your 'selves' match up to each one.
- For most people, a portfolio career will be more likely to satisfy a wider range of 'selves' than other career patterns.

Notes
55 Mr Benn © 2009 David McKee. Mr Benn is used courtesy of David McKee by arrangement with Clive Juster & Associates.
56 *Working Identity: Unconventional Strategies for Reinventing Your Career* (Harvard Business School Press, 2003).
57 Hazel Marcus & Paula Nurius, 'Possible Selves', *American Psychologist*, 41, No 9, (1986): 954–969.

Step 6

My networks

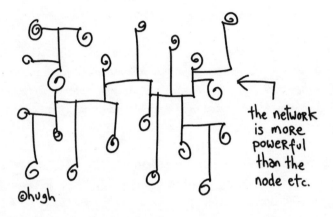

the network is more powerful than the node etc.

©hugh

'Networking is making the most of the people you meet to your mutual advantage.' Carole Stone (*Networking: The Art of Making Friends*)

'Where do I start?' Not surprisingly, that's a frequently asked question.

'I don't know anyone in the catering/education/IT/engineering/home-made crafts industry'. This is great news. Great because if you did, you would most likely pin all your hopes and expectations on them and their willingness to find you a job/project and stop taking *responsibility* yourself.

It's very similar to having an agent (which Katie once had). 'He said he could help boost my career because he knew all the important people. I stopped trying so hard to market myself and no jobs ever materialized.'

Katie learned the hard way that no one will ever 'sell' you the way that you do. One exception to this is if you're able to inspire what Ken Blanchard[58] calls 'raving fans'. These are people you've worked for and are so impressed by what you've done that they rave about you to others. They don't do this for money, just the knowledge that you will again do great work and they'll be recognised for knowing talented people. This is an ideal place to be – but how to get there?

'When you retrace the steps of highly successful people, you see a similar pattern. It's not the path they follow, where they go, or the speed they travel. It's that they're not travelling alone. They make friends along the way that help them stay on track: they network.' UpMo[59]

What has networking ever done for us?

Well, apart from meeting new people, exploring ideas, getting work, sharing experiences, finding new resources, accessing money, solving problems, joining a likeminded community and helping us create jobs that allow us to work flexibly, earn well and contribute to exciting projects – not much.

Stop thinking that networking is something special and just start to enjoy meeting new people. Remember you can always continue the conversation online if they turn out to be brilliant. Or, alternatively, you never have to see them again if you don't want to. Clay Shirky, the author of *Here Comes Everybody: The Power of Organizing Without Organizations*, a book which discusses the role of technology in the formation and experience of groups, says:

'The best tool ever invented for improving communication is the table. Online tools aren't better than face-to-face contact, they're just better than nothing.'[60]

We're both passionate about creating and maintaining relationships online. Indeed, we believe we're only just beginning to see what's possible with web communication. But first, let's consider the real face-to-face stuff.

Start here...

Cast your mind back to Step 3: My motivated skills. 'A motivated skill is unlearned, genetic, linked to our temperament, something we're born with. It dictates how we prefer to behave.' From that definition, these motivated skills stay with us for all of our lives and we can choose whether or not we use them for our work. So when looking for a 'job' to add to your portfolio, a good exercise could be to talk about your motivated skills with a friend or trusted work colleague. Just talking about your achievements and the skills you've used to make these happen can be a liberating experience in itself.

Career expert Bernard Haldane[61], when teaching his courses, would, after just one day of getting people to explore their achievements, identifying their skills and vocalising them, send participants out of the classroom 'to find a job'. They were asked to approach people they'd never met and say:

'Hello. I need some advice. I don't expect you to have a job for me or even know of one, but I'm looking. Would you please look over this report on my capabilities and give me your ideas on work that might match my strengths?'

It was amazing to hear what kind of positive feedback the students received. Why? Because generally people like to help others if they can. Everyone has their own unique network of contacts and friends they can call on. This technique is so simple yet not many people think to use it. Is it laziness? Fear of rejection? Fear of failure? Or maybe even fear of success?

'Many individuals would rather not know what is strong about them, the strengths that point to growth and reveal potential. A greater degree of responsibility is required to take hold of success rather than to stay in the safe area of complacency and complaint.' Bernard Haldane

A chief technology officer at a multi-national electronics company with whom Katie recently worked said he started his technology career in the city by creating a CV of achievements. He then went round in person to all the companies he wanted to work for. He asked to see either the HR director or CTO so he could personally hand it in and, of course, tell them about his motivated skills. Most of the time he was told to send in his CV but he said he didn't have the funds to send in so many copies (this was before widespread access to e-mail), so was delivering by foot. Several weeks and 35 companies later, he had nine job offers to choose from. Was it luck? We don't think so. His story reminds us of what the legendary golfer Gary Player said: 'The harder I work, the luckier I get.'

Talk to people, especially those you don't know. If you're not sure what specific job you want to do, they may be able to look at your achievements and see possibilities that you don't. They may even suggest work arenas that you hadn't even thought of. Part of Katie's portfolio is now creating business stories and designing presentation slides. She works with professional designers and great design has become part of her business offering. If someone had told her she'd be doing this a couple of years ago, she wouldn't have believed them. She even thought for a long time that she wasn't creative.[62] How many self-limiting beliefs do you have? Have you actually tried to do something you might well enjoy but believe you're no good at?

'Networking is the whole essence of who I am. I love finding out about other people and they ask about me.' Karen Cannard

Think more about *connecting* with interesting people. Somehow it sounds easier than networking. Remember that you can mine your existing networks.

- **Family** – talk to them about your strengths and achievements. These are the people who know you best. Be as open and honest with them as you can. Remember, this is a start of a new period of your life and you need to embrace a completely new way of thinking about how you'll spend the rest of your working life. Don't rule out anything at this stage. What do you enjoy doing? What activities give you energy? Can you do any of these and get paid even a small amount? Talking to your family like this will also help them to see you in a different light.

- **Friends** also know you well. They can give you feedback from a different angle. Do they see any qualities in you that you don't see? Are any of them doing something you might be interested in? Can they connect a few dots for you?

  'I really enjoy meeting people. Every time you interact with someone it's a possible business opportunity. And some of them actually become good friends as well.' Lisa Milnor

- **Work colleagues** can be useful but be careful who you speak to as this may be misconstrued. You want to be in a position of strength before you make any career decisions. Talking about other career options may be interpreted as you not showing commitment to the job in hand.

- **Weak ties,** such as the person in the paper shop, on the train, at the hairdresser's, golf club, gym, networking and business events.

Never underestimate the value of these. Weak ties can be more useful than strong ones. This is because your strong ties (family and friends) probably know the same or mostly the same people as you do. The resources and access to information and people they have is likely to be pretty much the same as you have.

'More than 25 per cent of people who find jobs through networking receive the referral from someone they meet once a year or less.'[63]

People know people. People have personal networks – sometimes huge ones. It's useful in this situation to know and be able to talk about your motivated strengths. Grow your network by going to events and courses as you can.

'Do things that attract opportunities.' Oli Barrett, (connector, entrepreneur, speaker, writer, speed networker)

You may have a vague idea of the area you might like to work in. For example, it may be IT, media, teaching, HR, horticulture, writing, DIY, organic farming...almost all vocations have events, courses and work experience opportunities.

'I have had to live by networking as I'm self-employed. I enjoy it because there's an element of gossip in it. I like keeping in touch with people because "you never know".' Richard Maude

Networking events
'What do I say?' Where to start?

Be honest and open. If you're just trying out a few ideas, then say so. Explain why you were compelled to attend the event today and that you

So tell me something interesting about yourself. Lie if you have to.

(c)gapingvoid.com

hoped to be able to learn through the experience of others. Again, the motivated skills 'script' could be very useful here. To get the ball rolling, here are a couple of suggestions to get conversations started from people who have – in the nicest possible way – put themselves about a bit.

- 'Why are you here today?' Heather Jackson
- 'And what are you working on at the moment?' Oli Barrett
- 'Hi, my name is Steven. This is my first time at this event. Have you been to any of these before?'
- or at a hosted event, 'How do you know so and so?'
  Steven D'Souza, (author, networker, connector, speaker)

These suggestions work really well because they take the pressure off people having to explain and justify what they do by using a single title. The questions are designed so as to get the other person talking and to show that you're prepared to listen. When asked, 'What do you do?' there's pressure to come up with a single professional label and be instantly judged on your answer.

'I don't like networking. It always seems so false and I never know what to say' is a common cry from many people. We say the answer is to change the one thing we can all change if we so desire: our attitude. Believe something good will come out of it. There's usually at least one person who makes the event worthwhile for you. They've something positive to offer to you or you to them. Either way, you've started a conversation, which, if desired, can be continued online until you want to or can actually meet up again.

What is a great result?

What do you want from meeting new people? Some ideas on areas of work you might enjoy? A new job? A good contact?

Try to think what you'd like to get out of the experience. What looks like a good outcome for you? And can you 'give' anything in return?

There are many books dedicated to the art of networking. Two of the best are *Brilliant Networking* by Steven D'Souza[64] along with...*and death came third!* by Andy Lopata and Peter Roper[65]. That title, by the way, comes from research showing that of all the things that people fear the most walking into a room and a fear of strangers came first, public speaking came second and the title tells you the rest!

Steven D'Souza talks about a networking mindset, building your network, networking in practice and managing your network. Some of his great networking event tips are:

- When someone tells you his or her name, try to use it as soon as possible in the conversation. It will help you to remember it and the person feels valued.
- If a name is tricky to pronounce, ask the person how to say it or spell it. It can be a good conversation starter.
- Groups form early, so arrive on time when it's easier to start a conversation.
- If at a formal networking event, ask the host to smooth the way by introducing you to people you'll have something in common with.

- Listen carefully and ask thoughtful questions but try not to interrogate.
- When you connect people, say something about them as well as their name. 'This is Katie – she runs her own communications company; she specialises in getting people and businesses heard.'
- If you're talking with just one other person, don't leave them hanging there when you want to move on. End a conversation by introducing them to someone you've already met. 'I need to talk to X, can I introduce you to Y?'

Here are Andy Lopata's three tips.

1 Be courageous – ask for introductions.
2 Be committed – does your phone ring by itself?
3 Be patient – you don't know who they are.

He also talks about three tools.

1 Pursue the relationship, not the sale.
2 People are interested in people who are interested in them.
3 Ask for what you want.

Finally, he talks about making a good impression, the importance of keeping in touch and asking for feedback – which Katie knows he does personally because he asked her for feedback recently!

Speed networking

The clue is in the name. You spend just three minutes with a person – he or she tells you about him/herself and you tell them about yourself. It can be a bit hit and miss, but occasionally a person can introduce you to a useful contact once they know what line of work you're in. It's very much like speed dating: you may have to kiss a few frogs but a prince will eventually appear. This technique ensures you meet quite a few different people with the massive added benefit of trying your 'story' out many times (see Step 8: My story.)

Events

There's no shortage of events to go to. A good place to start is online. Just search, for example, for 'teaching + events' or 'organic farming + events' and a plethora of results will appear. It may be that you know about a publication, a magazine or newspaper that covers the area you want to explore. Many offer their own courses or events and this could be a good place to start. The additional benefit is that they often create a pre-event blog (online diary) telling you much more about who will be speaking, workshop details, demonstrations and what's still to be finalised.

They sometimes also offer delegates the opportunity to register their details and encourage online networking between the people who'll attend. You can then arrange to meet up during the event. The real value of these events is in who you meet, so make sure you talk to a wide range of people during the breaks.

Even if you don't get to talk directly to a speaker you admire, you may be able to e-mail them and say you attended and would be interested to find out more; could they recommend people and/or sites you could follow up?

'Life is so full of crossroads that you never know about unless you network.' Richard Maude

Taster/part-time courses

These can last from a couple of hours to a couple of weeks. This could be an option if you're thinking of including this activity as part of your portfolio.

There are many pluses including:

- they involve a short time commitment;
- they're inexpensive or free;
- you can make useful connections through them;
- you learn a new skill;
- you get to 'try on' a new you (see Step 5: My selves).

Longer/full-time courses

You need to be more certain that this is the course for you but it could be well worth the effort and expense if you need to make that bigger transition. You may need a qualification to be able to start to practise your chosen profession, but you could try to work in that arena before qualifying. For example, if you were training to become a physiotherapist, you might be able to work as a part-time receptionist in a physiotherapist practice where you'd meet people on a daily basis who were doing the work you would love to do. You could ask questions, see them working and possibly go to events with them.

Work experience

Katie once worked as a personal trainer in Hong Kong. One day, a TV crew descended on the health club where she was working and filmed a report all about how personal trainers were the latest and greatest thing to hit the former colony. Two weeks later, the report was aired – Katie thought it was dreadful. It didn't actually poke fun but it didn't exactly rave about the new service either. She can remember thinking, 'I'd like to be able to tell this story'.

The next day, she polished up her CV and headed to ATV, one of Hong Kong's then two English-language stations. Within a fortnight, she was standing in for one of the children's TV reporters. She had to be taught how to hold a microphone, how to interview, how to film pieces to camera, how to write for television and how pull it all together. It was hard work as she still had her personal training job but it was fun, exciting and thrilling to discover what she really wanted to do. The only downside was the money...£0. In fact, it cost *her*, as she had to pay to travel to locations and the studios.

Slowly, she started to improve and moved to the other station, TVB, where she got paid a very small amount but not enough to scrap her day job. A year later, she was offered the researcher's role as well as her reporting job, a bit more money and she also started to do jobs related to TV such as voice-overs and one-off presenting jobs. Katie left her health-club job and threw herself into what she really wanted to do – TV journalism. She tells this story only because she didn't realise that's what she wanted to do, but she knew she wanted to try it.

Herminial Ibarra[66] says,

'We learn who we are – in practice, not in theory – by testing reality, not by looking inside. We discover the true possibilities by doing – trying out new activities, reaching out to new groups, finding new role models and reworking our story as we tell it to those around us...To launch ourselves anew, we need to get out of our heads. We need to act.'

Offer to make the tea, answer the phone, hold the microphone, read the car park report on local radio (as Katie did). If you think you might enjoy it, work at it – literally.

'Networking for me is better than the ironing.' Richard Maude

Are you ready for networking?

Go to **www.upmo.com** profiler and use their free network readiness tool.

UpMo[67], with the support of Pepperdine University's Graziadio School of Business Management, in 2008 surveyed 637 professionals, who also elaborated on their responses during in-depth, personal interviews. 40 per cent said that they identified their current positions by leveraging relationships through either an existing network or the referral of a colleague or friend. A 2008 ExecuNet[68] study supports these findings, revealing that 70 per cent of participating executives found their current positions by networking.

The UpMo report also showed that professionals tend to network only if and when looking for their next positions. If you're a portfolio worker, networking has to be a way of life not something that you dip into if recession, redundancy or job boredom hits. The report highlighted that most people thought that the single most critical factor in determining the value of their networks was to develop deeper relationships with people already in their networks. The study demonstrated that this was a fallacy and that the key factor in successful networking was the breadth of connections with the right people – people willing to recommend you.

'If individuals within your network are not willing to recommend you, they are of no, and possibly even negative, value to your network. If individuals within your network – some of whom you may have developed deep relationships with – are not willing to recommend you and may even speak negatively about you, they in fact detract from the value of your network.'

They also found that 46 to 60 year olds spent three times as long networking as their younger colleagues. And before any Gen Ys comment that this is simply because older people are slower, that's not what the results show!

Who can help?

We are not alone. As we've briefly mentioned family, friends, work colleagues and 'weak ties' all help. But as we've discovered, it's not just about finding a promotional network. To be a successful portfolio worker you need at least four different kinds of support:

- emotional
- development
- promotional
- material

Emotional support comes from someone who:

- you can talk problems through with – a *confidante;*
- you can call on in a crisis – a *crisis manager;*
- makes you feel competent and valued. Someone who you can comfortably share good news with – a *validator;*
- you can take a break with, have a drink or a meal with to 'get away from it all', someone you can have a really good laugh with – an *escapist.*

Developmental support comes from someone who:

- is interested in you, what you want to achieve and wants to help you navigate your own journey of discovery – a *mentor.* Having someone who's personally interested in your development and achievements and wanting you to succeed can be enormously helpful. Sometimes it's not just for the information but having a person who can empathise with what you're going through and suggest ways of dealing with it.
- challenges you to sit up and take a good look at yourself. Someone who'll give truthful negative feedback that you need to hear – a *challenger.*

- knows how to get things done, who's practical and experienced – a *fixer*.
- is a specialist in your areas of interest – an *expert*.

Promotional support comes from someone who:

- introduces you to new ideas, new interests and new people – a *connector*. Malcolm Gladwell, author of *The Tipping Point*[69], describes connectors in this way:

  'What makes someone a connector? The first – and most obvious – criterion is that connectors know lots of people. They are the kinds of people who know everyone. All of us know someone like this. But I don't think that we spend a lot of time thinking about the importance of these kinds of people. I'm not even sure that most of us really believe that the kind of person who knows everyone really knows everyone. But they do.'

- knows you well enough to bring you together with a possible employer or contractor. They are looking for a win–win outcome – a *matchmaker*.
- helps to promote you and sell your skills – a *marketer*.

Material support comes from someone who:

- will help you out with practical support, e.g. use of equipment, premises, child minding, caring for relatives, etc. – *people*.
- will help you with banks, agencies, investors, individuals, business angels, etc. – *finance*.

Other support
Add any other kind of support that you think that you might require.

_____

_____

_____

Our support relationships can often rely on just one or two people. This can put a great deal of pressure on those individuals. Take a look at the Support Networks table below. Doing this will help you to identify what support you have now and what you might need going forwards. It's useful to include people with a range of competencies and experience. Remember that asking for support is a sign of strength. Too many of us lack the courage to ask, or see having to ask for help, as a weakness.

Go ahead and fill in the names of the people or institutions that currently provide your support.

CAN DO: My support networks

EMOTIONAL	Actual names	Possibles
Confidante		
Crisis manager		
Validator		
Escapist		

DEVELOPMENT		
Mentor		
Challenger		
Fixer		
Expert		
PROMOTIONAL		
Connector		
Matchmaker		
Marketer		
MATERIAL		
People		
Finance		
OTHER SUPPORT		

Review questions

1 Does anything surprise me when I review my Support Network table?

_____

_____

_____

2 Are there other kinds of support that are crucial to me but aren't listed in this table?

_____

_____

_____

3 Are there any gaps?

_____

_____

4 Do I rely on one or two people only for my support? Does it matter?

_____

_____

_____

5 What are the consequences for me and for them?

_____

_____

_____

6 Do I want to change my network in any way?

_____

_____

_____

7 What am I going to do to recruit people to my network?

_____

_____

_____

We suggest you list the people you want to recruit and note exactly what you're going to do to enlist them and by when.

Keep connecting

Big list of contacts. Small amount of time. Look at the names you've listed in your network. They may be people you speak to every day but others maybe you only talk to once in a while. We urge you to think again. These are the people who can help you to create and grow your portfolio career. They may not bring work directly to you but they're highly influential and, if convinced and gently reminded of your talents and abilities, they'll willingly promote, develop and support you in any way they can.

One of the best ways of doing this is to send via e-mail, short, interesting articles or sites that you think they personally will enjoy or engage with. It doesn't take long. When you see something that might interest them, just click the 'send via e-mail button' with a quick note along the lines of:

'Hi Mike, saw this and thought of you. Warm regards, Barrie.*'*

This helps you to stay in touch and also to be of some service to the other person. If they're seeking work, you might be able to put them in touch with someone in your network. That truly is an excellent feeling. Also, if you do a great piece of work, write an article or discover a new way to help your clients, don't be shy. Maybe just put as a PS at the bottom of the e-mail or a hyperlink to your blog or website where they can read a little more about it (see Step 9: My brand). The emphasis is on 'little': people want to know what you're doing but they don't always have much time.

When someone does something nice for you, send a thank-you note. One of the best ways of doing this is by sending a real card by snail mail. We know it's old fashioned but because so few people now do it, it really sets you apart and makes the person receiving it feel special.

World-renowned author and speaker Brian Tracy[70] suggests being a 'go-giver' rather than a go-getter. He says:

'Someone has observed that no one ever built a statue to a person to acknowledge what he or she got out of life. Statues are built only to people to acknowledge what they gave. The most powerful, influential and successful people you will ever meet always look for ways to do nice things for others. When you meet someone under almost any circumstance, one of the best questions you can ask is this: 'Is there anything that I can do for you?' Always look for ways to put in rather than to take out. The successful man or woman of today is a "go-giver" as well as a go-getter.'

He goes on to say: 'Take time to really listen to people, especially your staff and co-workers. The more and better you listen to others, the greater is your influence.'

Katie has been having horse riding lessons for some time now (getting better slowly). To get a horse to move at its best, you ask it to come on the 'bit' where it will be most responsive to doing whatever you ask. She was using the reins to take and the bit to give and not getting very far. Nic, her riding teacher, suggested the horse might respond better the other way.

'Give first and then take back.'

Katie tried it. And you know what? It works every time.

Over-egging the Webtastic pudding?

'For individuals and small producers, this may be the birth of a new era, perhaps even a golden one, on a par with the Italian

Renaissance or the rise of Athenian democracy.' Don Tapscott and Anthony Williams[71]

Wow! That's a bold statement. And while we think it may be over-egging the Webtastic pudding, we understand why the authors are so excited. Books that feature portfolio careers and were written little more than a decade ago barely even mention using a computer. We forget how far we've come in such a short time. We think what the *Wikinomics* authors are trying to say is that we're at the beginning of a wonderful journey, one that'll allow pretty much all of us, regardless of education, social background, wealth, race, gender and ability to be able to connect and have a conversation with almost any individual or organisation on the planet. That's another wow!

If we aren't alone in the real world, then we won't be alone online for very long. We live in interesting times. No generation in human history has so much information, comment and analysis that we have. Have a look at the 'Shift Happens'[72] video. The original (it has spawned many variations) has been viewed millions of times. If you haven't seen it, we strongly urge you to invest around five minutes of your time. It's worth it and puts into context some of the paradigm shifts we're seeing right now, including:

- The US Dept of Labor predicts today's students will have 10 to 14 jobs by the age of 38.
- The amount of technical information is doubling every two years. By 2010, it's predicted to double every *72 hours*. For students starting a four-year degree, half of what they learn is outdated by year three.
- The amount of unique information generated in 2008 is the equivalent of that generated in the previous 5,000 years.
- There are 175 million Facebook users and 110 million MySpace users worldwide.

- There are 31 million searches on Google every day.
- In 1992, the first text message was sent. In 2008, there were more text messages sent than the population of the entire planet.
- It took 38 years for the radio to hit a target audience of 50 million, 13 years for TV to hit that target, four years for the Internet, three years for the iPod, and two years for Facebook.
- We are preparing students for jobs that don't yet exist, using technology that hasn't been invented in order to solve problems we don't know are problems yet.

'We can't solve problems by using the same kind of thinking we used when we created them'. Albert Einstein

What does all this mean to portfolio workers? It means that by embracing the digital world, we dramatically increase and strengthen our networks, gain unlimited access to information and most importantly, continue to invest in our own education and growth.

Almost a quarter of the world's population uses the Internet. In Europe, it's almost 50 per cent; in the US almost 75 per cent and in Australasia 60 per cent.[73]

So information is important. Very important. But what happens when we all have almost equal access to the same information? It becomes about relevance and meaning. The people who'll succeed in this new economy will be those who can make sense and condense this information. 'Google' may now be a verb, but it still can't make that information relevant to a particular situation. It's getting better but at the moment, it still needs us to do the final bit. The brilliance of a service like Google is that:

'Google provides a platform and network that enables others to succeed – and when they succeed, so does Google.'[74]

It helps others to succeed and in the process, we succeed too. This is particularly important to remember when we're trying to find people who can help us, people who share the same interests and passions. The Web is a great tool to enable us to either start relationships or to continue them. We can even have meaningful relationships with people we've never met and may never meet. This means we don't have to limit ourselves to physical boundaries: we literally have a worldwide audience to talk to and play with.

Social networks

LinkedIn, Facebook, MySpace, Plaxo, MSN and Bebo are just some of the most popular social networks with literally millions of users. They can be good ways of connecting with like-minded individuals and of course hooking into their own personal networks. LinkedIn[75], for example, is more business-oriented.It has more than 38 million registered users spanning 170 industries. The site quite openly states the number and type of people linked to each individual. It also details what these people actually do for a living, lists their CV, interests and hobbies. Uber-Marketer Guy Kawasaki[76] has some great tips on how to get the best out of using it. Essentially, it's not just about being able to contact people – you can now e-mail the British Prime Minister through his No. 10 website[77] – but it's about making yourself heard and having the person you want to contact, want to contact you too.

According to recruitment consultancy Harvey Nash, networking sites catapult careers. It says: 'Networking sites are not career suicide – they can actually be used to nurture career progression.'

In a 2008 survey, Harvey Nash found that 90 per cent of senior executives are increasingly turning to professional networking sites such as LinkedIn to progress their careers. It's a figure that compares to just half posting their CV on a job board. In addition, 93 per cent of executives claim that investing time and effort into developing a strong personal brand is important to them and their career.

While 74 per cent of respondents believe that actively building a personal brand offline is the most popular method for progressing their career, social and professional networking sites take second place with over two thirds of senior executives actively using their network to develop their personal brand. When searching for a job via a social networking site, most senior executives would look to LinkedIn first (57 per cent) and Plaxo second (16 per cent) with Facebook only coming in at fifth place (6 per cent).

Cristina Hoole, European marketing director at LinkedIn, says: 'As competition in the global job market intensifies, it has become essential for executives, at all levels, to build and strengthen their personal profiles online. This research reaffirms our own understanding that professional networking sites already play an increasingly important role in helping candidates stay well connected and career-informed.' [78]

Both Facebook and MySpace (albeit it to a slightly lesser extent) perform the same functions. They are less business-focused and more true social networks but we know people who virtually (in every sense of the word) run their businesses through Facebook and are being highly successful.

The UpMo[79] research described earlier refers to 'networking noise'. The authors claim that networking in today's connected world isn't as easy as it seems, despite a plethora of online tools that help us visualise the social graph.

'Unfortunately, these tools also tend to give the impression that LinkedIn "connections" or Facebook "friends" signify valuable relationships. If only it were so simple. In reality though, networking today is more challenging, more complex than it ever has been: there are more relationships to manage and put into context; more unwanted e-mails and requests to answer; more items, neither urgent

nor important, on our to-do lists. Our burgeoning contact lists have birthed an aversion to networking and more "networking noise" than the added exposure and opportunity they were meant to create. This is why truly effective networking – networking in the manner of the high earning and high career-level elite professionals represented within this study – requires more than "connections" or "friends"; it requires cutting through clutter and focusing on what matters – real, mutually beneficial partnerships.'

Explore your work fantasies...

...and any 'crazy' career options that you've thought about in your lifetime. 'I always wanted to be a...'; 'I think it would be fun to work in...'. Let your imagination run riot. We know a very intelligent technology consultant who worked for a big-name company for many years until he got bored with the travel and decided it was time to do something else. He thought making films would be fun and so started up his own production company. It was a steep learning curve because he had no formal production training but he did succeed and now creates films, mainly for large technology businesses.

Some companies are starting to help their people explore opportunities. Google takes exploration very seriously. Each employee can use 20 per cent of work time to do what he or she wishes. They can learn a new skill, try out a new idea or let their mind go to where they want to be. There's a compelling reason for all this corporate altruism: 50 per cent of new products, including Gmail and Google News, came from this '20 per cent time'. Forward-thinking businesses are increasingly using a win–win approach to retain their best talent.

We urge you to explore more about how you can benefit from using technology. Dr Scott McLeod, the co-creator of the wildly popular Shift Happens video, suggests we are in the early transition phase moving into something that's radically different. For example, he sees:

1 a computing device in every kid's (and educator's) hand, 24/7;
2 ubiquitous high-speed wireless access to the Internet regardless of where you are;
3 a much greater emphasis on individualised, personalised, creative learning;
4 higher-order thinking rather than low-level fact regurgitation.

We rather like this vision of the near future, especially points three and four where we feel portfolio workers are already on board.

We'll return and expand on this theme in Step 9: My brand, where we'll discuss how to use the Web to its greatest advantage so that people will be able to find you and hear you. But we want to end this Step with another piece of Carole Stone wisdom, which is very simple. She ultimately says about networking and connecting:

'Take a chance...you never know.'

'You never know' has become a mantra for us both. We use it before making any decision if we're uncertain about the value of accepting a particular invitation, attending an event or writing a piece for someone or something.

Having said that, we do of course sometimes say 'no'...

Summary
You've:

- explored the meaning of networking.
- examined how to mine existing networks.
- looked at maximising the benefits from events, courses and work experience.

- identified your own support network and named the people who provide you with emotional, developmental, promotional and material support.
- started to see how IT and social media can contribute enormously to your career networking (much more in Step 9: My brand).

Notes

58 *Raving Fans: A Revolutionary Approach to Customer Service* (William Morrow, 1993).

59 Upwardly Mobile, known as UpMo, describe themselves as an online career 'GPS' that guides professionals through the daily decisions and actions that shape success. **www.upmo.com**

60 Interview with Clay Shirky in 'Online Information', *Guardian* supplement, November 2008.

61 *Career Satisfaction & Success: A Guide to Job and Personal Freedom* (Jist Works Inc., 1996).

62 She had clearly forgotten about the design prize that she won in school aged seven – and of course the tragedy is that's exactly the kind of thing that we forget or more to the point is plastered over by negative comments or experiences.

63 Trinity College, University of Dublin, Careers Advisory Service.

64 *Brilliant Networking: What the Best Networkers Know, Do and Say* (Pearson, 2008). See also **www.brilliantnetworking.net**.

65 *...and death came third! The Definitive Guide to Networking and Speaking in Public* (Lean Marketing Press, 2006).

66 *Working Identity: Unconventional Strategies for Reinventing Your Career* (Harvard Business School Press, 2004).

67 Professional Networking and Career Advancement report, 2009.

68 ExecuNet's Executive Job Market Intelligence report, 2008.

69 *The Tipping Point* (Abacus, 2002).

70 **www.briantracy.com**

71 Don Tapscott & Anthony Williams, *Wikinomics* (Atlantic Books, 2007).

72 **www.youtube.com/watch?v=jpEnFwiqdx8**

73 **www.internetworldstats.com**

74 Jeff Jarvis (from *Media Guardian*, 9 February 2009)

75 **www.linkedin.com**

76 **http://blog.linkedin.com/2007/07/25/ten-ways-to-use./**

77 **www.number10.gov.uk**

78 **www.sociallyminded.co.uk/2008/07/official-we-are-a-big-jobsite-says-linkedin/**

79 Professional Networking and Career Advancement report, 2009.

Step 7

My portfolio

> 'I recommend managing your career as a portfolio of experiences and competencies that diversify you. Based on your strengths, interests and level of risk tolerance, you make career moves that fit your long- and short-term goals. You choose opportunities that stretch and expand your skills instead of focusing only on grabbing the next title on the rung. You find security in being in control of each move, rather than feeling at the mercy of your boss, your company or the economy to decide your fate.' Nina Ham[80]

You are now well on your way to creating a portfolio career for yourself. You've discovered:

1 whether or not this work style is right for you;

2 how you'll finance yourself;

3 your motivated skills – the skills you must use to feel alive and fulfilled;

4 your values – your ultimate litmus test before deciding whether or not to take on any job or piece of work;

5 how many different selves you possess and which ones you wish to focus on;

6 the full range of your networks and the types of support you need and that you can rely on.

It's now time to begin to populate your career portfolio.

It's worth thinking about the origins of the word 'portfolio'. It comes from the 18th-century Italian word *portafoglio* and refers to the large carrying case that artists used to contain and to display their work. The contents would continually change as their work developed, sponsors were switched, new techniques and technologies were discovered and the artists themselves matured and wished to explore new facets of themselves and their work.

CAN DO: What's in your portfolio?

Some of you will already have more than one job and will have listed those in earlier chapters. Some of you will have just the one job and are considering a portfolio career. To help you work out which skills you're using, take your present job and split it up into its component parts. For example, David is a restaurant manager and when he did this activity, he discovered that his job consisted of:

• front-of-house work with customers;

• ordering food and drink;

• dealing and negotiating with suppliers;

- managing the staff schedules;
- managing the staff
- administration – bills, VAT, staff gratuities, absence sheets, etc.;
- evaluating feedback from customers;
- planning menus with the chef;
- reporting back on systems and results to the owner;
- hiring new and temporary staff;
- checking out the competition;
- attending training courses.

He worked out what percentage of his time was spent in each activity. Then he rated each activity from 1 to 10 according to how much he enjoyed doing it. The results surprised him.

ACTIVITY	percentage of TIME	percentage of ENJOYMENT
Front-of-house work with customers	35	9
Ordering food and drink	3	3
Dealing and negotiating with suppliers	3	6
Managing the staff schedules	3	4
Managing the staff	20	7
Administration	20	4
Evaluating feedback from customers	2	8
Planning menus with the chef	5	8
Reporting back to the owner	2	7
Hiring new and temporary staff	3	7
Checking out the competition	2	9
Attending training courses	2	9

David discovered that what he enjoyed most was the customer contact and getting customer feedback. He was quite entrepreneurial so liked checking out the competition and also loved learning new things but rarely got any time for that. The admin tasks were a real chore along with the mechanics of ordering supplies. He clearly enjoyed the creativity involved in working with the chef but this took up too little of his time.

From this analysis, he decided that he'd do better if he was a part-time *maître d'* at the restaurant and was able to negotiate this with the owner. His first portfolio job was therefore *maître d'* for four nights a week. Having completed his motivated skills and values activities and looked at his range of 'selves' over the next 12 months, David negotiated two more part-time jobs. He became a temporary manager moving from restaurant to restaurant for two to three days a week, which made good use of his people management skills but meant reduced administration. In addition, he went into partnership with two ex-chefs who'd set up a website selling specialised Italian food. He got involved in sourcing the products, travelling to Italy to do so. He also went along to food exhibitions, which he loved.

In this way you can see how analysing a full-time job can help you to identify the parts of it that you want to do more of and those parts that you wish to do less of. Try it for yourself opposite.

ACTIVITY	percentage of TIME	percentage of ENJOYMENT

On the basis of your reflections write in what you would like more of, less of and what you would like to keep the same in work life right now.

MORE OF	LESS OF	KEEP THE SAME

CAN DO: Other jobs you've done

Having analysed your current job, you should now do the same for other jobs that you've had.

Make a list of these jobs in the table overleaf and give each one an overall rating for how much you enjoyed the job overall from 1 to 10.

Jobs I've held	Overall enjoyment

On separate pieces of paper now deconstruct each of these in the way that you did it in the previous activity.

You might want to refer back to Step 3. How many of your motivated skills are you using now?

Are there any common threads that you can identify that run through many of your jobs that you've enjoyed? Similarly, are there negative themes that you can identify?

Write them down here.

Positive threads are:

_____

_____

_____

_____

Negative themes are:

_____

_____

_____

_____

CAN DO: What do I love to do in my spare time?

You'll have done many things other than paid work. Barrie wrote poetry, stories for his children and grandchildren, played and watched cricket, chaired his local community association, ran in charity runs, mentored a number of people who were starting out or reinventing themselves, cooked and enjoyed experimenting with new recipes, raised funds for community projects, was a member of a wine group and continually learned more about wines, set up his own blog, designed and produced his own newsletters. If he were to list these, what kind of revenue-producing possibilities might emerge for him? We came up with the following:

How about writing short stories, working as a chef, charging for mentoring and coaching, fundraising for a commission, producing newsletters for customers, running wine- and food-tasting evenings at a local club or restaurant for profit?

Below, list what you do or have done in your spare time and rate them from 1 to 10 for enjoyment. In the final column, think of a job that you could do with the skills, values and interests that have driven you to do these activities.

ACTIVITIES	ENJOYMENT RATING	POSSIBLE JOB

Remember that you might not want to turn an interest or unpaid work into a revenue stream but it certainly makes sense to check it out.

CAN DO: Mind mapping your way to revenue

In Step 6, hopefully you'll have identified a mentor or possibly a connector. Now is the time to get her or him actively involved.

Mind mapping is a form of brainstorming on paper or online invented by Tony Buzan.

The Mind Map™ method:

- can contain masses of diverse but interconnected ideas with the main themes clearly defined;
- can ease the task of selecting priorities and areas to work on while seeing the 'big picture';
- offers more coherence while being easy to add to or expand;
- closely resembles the way our brainsare wired.

Before you do this next exercise, it might be useful for you to review this Step's CAN DOs and also look back at your lists of motivated skills and work values.

Then, working on a large sheet of paper, put the title of your mind map – My Portfolio Career – right at the centre.

To that centre add the heading for the first of the possible revenue themes that occur to you – think in terms of branch lines leaving the mainline stations and heading outwards to suburbs. Start anywhere with any topic. Write the theme heading in capitals or in a particular colour. For a more detailed description of how to use the technique go to **www.mindtools.com/pages**

The mind map that we've reproduced here is a genuine one by a recently graduated Gen Y-er exploring what he might want to do. What's interesting about his mind map is the vast range of possibilities open to

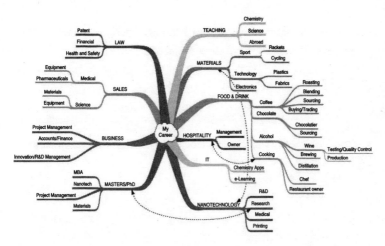

him. He could launch himself in any one of at least five directions. He could also try to combine some of his interests and skills, if he could find one job that would encompass them all. Almost certainly, he'll have difficulty in doing so and therefore is an obvious candidate for a portfolio career[81].

If you really want to do mind mapping on your computer, the one piece of software that Tony Buzan himself recommends can be found at **www.imindmap.com** and will cost you about £50. Interestingly, Tony himself, although endorsing this product, prefers the tactile experience of working up a map on paper. There are a number of freeware versions around if you Google them.

Reflecting on the different job ideas that occur to you, let your mind flow around each theme and develop your line of thought leading outwards. As thoughts come to mind, enter the key words on the line.

Think through and build your mind map around the different job ideas. Take your time: it's valuable work. When you've completed your mind map, study it carefully and as you do write in your thoughts on the following:

- What did I become aware of or what occurred to me as I compiled my portfolio career mind map?

_____

_____

_____

_____

- Which of my motivated skills would drive me towards particular jobs?

_____

_____

_____

_____

- Which of my work values would push me into the direction of the jobs I've brainstormed?

_____

_____

_____

_____

- Which of my selves do I really want to focus on?

_____

_____

_____

_____

- Who in my support network may help me to get these jobs?

_____

_____

_____

_____

Tips for managing your career portfolio

'I would like the relative safety of a company life but it can't fulfill all my needs. I need to have the flexibility to change – the freedom to drop stuff and start something else.' Chris Nel

- Don't just think about the present. Spend some time thinking about where you might want to be and what you might want to be doing five years from now. Step 10 provides you with an activity for doing this on page 201.
- Are there competencies that you'd like to develop, experiences you'd like to have, places you'd like to work, organisations you'd like to work in?
- Say 'yes' to things that expand your portfolio and 'no' to single-track career moves. Every time you say 'yes' to one thing, you'll need to say 'no' to something else. So if you take on assignments, projects, education, training or even a new role, you have to be sure that you're saying 'yes' because it expands your portfolio. Don't be tempted to say 'yes' just because something is offered to you. This can be a very difficult thing to do, especially if money is short.
- What do you need to learn to be able to populate your portfolio in the way that you want?
- Nina Ham[82] talks about knowing your 'most profitable competencies'. We talk about motivated skills but we're all discussing the same thing. She says:

'You can recession-proof your career by knowing exactly what your strongest competencies are and communicating them clearly. Instead of feeling stuck in your field or industry, look at what you do well that adds value. These are your most profitable competencies...the things other employers and departments want to bring in to their groups. By knowing and being able to communicate your best competencies, you are able to stay flexible and fill a wider number of roles in a wider variety of industries.'

• Keep up with social and technological trends. Sign up for the appropriate Google Alerts for the business areas you're interested in (see Step 9: My brand). Read the papers, trawl the Net, go to networking events and attend conferences and courses. In this way, you'll always be able to position yourself to potential employers and contractors within a business context that impresses and makes sense to them.

• If you watched the YouTube video on 'Shift Happens' referred to in Step 6, you'll recall that China will soon become the No. 1 English-speaking country in the world. That the top 10 jobs that will be in demand in 2010 didn't even *exist* in 2004. And that the amount of new information generated in the coming year is estimated to exceed all the information generated in the past 5,000 years. What are the implications for you? Simply that there's a greater chance than ever before that you can create a job for yourself as the world of work gets more malleable and transitory.

'If you stay in your field, you get locked into old thinking. Sixty per cent of innovation in diverse fields was made by outsiders in the first year they entered the field.' Jim Wilson

• Whatever you plan to do, make sure that you can use a computer and the main software packages. Understand how to use the Internet to get information and knowledge and for research. Practise using social networking sites, especially ones like LinkedIn, Facebook and Plaxo (see Step 9). You may need to learn how to set up a blog or website depending on your career objectives. Without these skills, it's difficult enough to get even a single-track or a serial career these days. For a portfolio career, it can make the challenge nigh impossible for you.

- Actively seek references and testimonials. If you use LinkedIn, you'll have an opportunity of inviting people who know you and your work to give you an online reference. But in addition to online references, just ask for e-mailed or written references and testimonials that you can add to your portfolio. Not sure how to ask? Try this:

'As you probably know I'm a portfolio worker. For me to continue to be successful, referrals and testimonials are my lifeblood. This means that I have to work particularly hard to ensure that my clients, like you, are truly satisfied with the work that I've done for you. In this way, hopefully, you may refer me on to other people. Would you be prepared to help me in this way?'

As we keep saying, most people like to help. But you should always try to get references right after the completed work so that your customer is clear about your contributions.

- The careers specialist Dianna Podmoroff[83] suggests creating and maintaining a success journal. She makes the point that the time to start thinking about your accomplishments and skills is not when you're looking for a new job. You need to be proactive and make a continuous inventory of what you do really well, the accolades you've been given and the noteworthy results you've been responsible for. Employers want to know what you'll do for them. When you have a ready list of things you've done, it is much easier to recall your most relevant achievements and skills. Her suggestions are:

- track your duties, projects and results;
- keep a list of professional development activities you've done;
- list the training you've completed;
- note your volunteer work;
- file any performance reviews you've been given and the written letters and e-mails you receive that note your performance.

She concludes by making the excellent point that one additional pay-off from this exercise is that in difficult times it's very affirming, boosting your confidence and self-esteem.

Causer, Deszca and Mazerolle[84] claim that to minimise risks a portfolio worker needs to develop a set of clients that, in effect, mirror your skill sets. They categorise these clients into three different types.

- **Money clients** provide the money needed to pay the bills. The skills used for these clients are generally not particularly unique or valuable. Individuals have these clients out of necessity not choice. Little learning takes place when doing work for money clients.

- **Learning clients** provide opportunities to learn new skills and concepts. Doing these activities the individual learns the skill set, which will provide him/her with the 'next generation' of skills to market. Generally, concrete or extrinsic rewards are not the focus of these skills. If payment is made, it will be for results since the individual is learning on the job and developing their skills as they work.

- **Niche clients** result from the matching of developed skills with a significant need. Here the individual can market or sell his/her skill at an appropriate price. Niche clients also allow you to develop your reputation and network for future work.

'Any one job can only fulfill part of what I look for in my work.'
Chris Nell

'I think it's easier for women to find different jobs.' Veronique Jaquard

CAN DO: Populating your portfolio

This is where you review all of your work in this Step and define a number of areas of paid work that you'd like to pursue. List them below and each one ask yourself:

1 Could I pursue this one immediately? Or in six months, one year, two years or longer?
2 Do I need to train or learn more to pursue this?
3 What revenue could I expect from this one?
4 Is this consistent with my values? Score 1 to 10 with 10 being the maximum and top score.
5 Will this help me to use my greatest motivated skills? Score 1 to 10 with 10 being the maximum.
6 Which of my 'selves' will this satisfy? (There may well be more than one.)

Job/Work	Time?	Training?	£££	Values	Skills	Selves

You're now looking at a potential portfolio of job, work and career opportunities.

How does this look to you? Are you excited, fearful, anxious or desperate to make a start?

Using motivated skills to find work

Deciding what you want to do is one thing, but getting a job or jobs consistent with your values and your motivated skills is something else. This is where we return to Bernard Haldane once more.

One of Bernard's motives for developing his system was to give people of all ages practical techniques that would help them to find jobs. Once you know your motivated skills, you can present them to a possible employer with examples that immediately convey your capabilities. Employers usually like people to be clear about their strengths and what they can bring to the organisation. David Marriott, who we quoted earlier, is convinced that he got his job with Harley-Davidson because he could describe his motivated skills and he discussed them in his interview.

Bernard had a four-step process, which was taught to thousands of people, mostly in the US.

- Step 1 was to get people to hear about your motivated skills and your potential.
- Step 2 was to get them to remember you for some time – two months or more.
- Step 3 was to encourage them to refer you to others who would also remember and refer you.
- Step 4 was to work that growing network of people as it would be those individuals who'd facilitate your job offers.

He taught people about 'informational interviewing' where you ask someone for half an hour of their time so that you can find out about the type of work they do or what's available in their organisation. You make it very clear you're researching and not looking for a job, which immediately takes the pressure off people. Once you've described your skills, more often than not people will try to think of others whom they know who may have something of interest to you. You then go to the next interviews with a personal recommendation.

These techniques still work effectively today although they haven't been widely taught in the UK. They can certainly be used to help you to create your portfolio career.

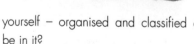

It's also worth considering taking the concept of a portfolio career quite literally at this point, too. When job hunting, you could actually take a portfolio with you – maybe a ring binder or something more creative. In this you should have as much information as possible about yourself – organised and classified and easy to find. What should be in it?

- Your story or stories (see Step 8).
- A list of your motivated skills.
- A list of your values.
- A statement of why you want to pursue a portfolio career. Check with the Introduction and also what your scores in Step 1 say about yourself.
- A traditional CV with an employment and educational history – but never start with that unless pushed.
- A list of your accomplishments, awards, performance reviews, etc.

- Samples of any work that you've done – articles, photographs of what you may have made or created, brochures, presentations that you've made. You might even have some CDs or DVDs that show what you can do.
- Testimonials, references and letters of support.

However much you place in your actual portfolio, this isn't something that you would open to allow potential employers to rummage through. In fact, you would probably benefit from sending them appropriate paperwork or examples of work in advance. You may also want to ensure that you have copies of key documents to leave with them. The advantage of having your portfolio with you is that if you're suddenly asked for evidence of something that you couldn't have predicted, then you may have something that you can put your hands on to show them.

Yes, but...don't you also have to have some luck?

In one of Barrie's earlier books[85], he states that 'luck is the crossroads where opportunity and preparation meet'. There's no doubt that un-planned events happen in all of our lives but we always have a choice as to how we respond. A fascinating book by Richard Wiseman[86] reports on his study of 400 exceptionally 'lucky' and also 'unlucky' people. Perhaps not surprisingly, he found that people who thought they were lucky tended to share the same attitudes and behaviour. Their unlucky counterparts exhibited the opposite.

'Lucky people' maximised chance opportunities; they used their intuition; they expected to be lucky and expected positive outcomes; their attitude allowed them to turn bad luck into good. When things weren't going well for them, they moved quickly to take control of the situation.

Yes, but...is it too late to radically to change the way I work?

We've interviewed people from 24 to 66 who've all made the decision to create a portfolio career. As you've no idea how long you're likely to live, other than that longevity is increasing by five hours a day[87] for people in the UK, then surely it can never be too late? Tom Kirkwood likes to say 'Welcome to the 29 hour day'. Research is now telling us for each day we live we gain another five hours at the end of our lives. What are we going to do with that extra time?

Ken Robinson says it's never too late to change our minds:[88]

'One of the most basic reasons for thinking that it's not too late to be who you are truly capable of being is the belief that life is linear. As if we are on a busy one-way street, we think we have no alternative but to keep going forward. If we missed something the first time, we can't double back and take another look because it takes all of our efforts to keep up with the traffic.'

All of the recent evidence we have on how our brains work, how we age and how our attitudes form and re-form, suggests that our lives aren't linear and we do ourselves a gross disservice by behaving as if they are. It really is never too late...

'You don't get to choose how you're going to die. Or when. You can only decide how you're going to live. Now.' Joan Baez

Yes, but...I don't have enough experience.
'Orville Wright didn't have a pilot's licence.'[89]

Says it all really.

Summary
You've:

- explored what activities are already in your existing job or jobs.
- examined your non-paid work and leisure activities to see if you can find any paid-work options.
- used mind mapping to identify possible jobs.
- looked at a variety of tips for managing a portfolio career.
- considered how you can use your motivated skills to get job offers.

Notes

80 www.successfromtheinsideout.com/library.html
81 His name is Richard Papworth Smith, recently graduated in Chemistry and Management and who, as we write, is still searching for what to do and where to start. Anyone who would like to make contact can do so at **rpapworthsmith@gmail.com**.
82 www.successfromtheinsideout.com
83 Dianna Podmoroff writes for the Mind Tools Career Excellence Club. To contact Dianna, email **Customer.Helpdesk@mindtools.com**
84 Tupper Cawsey, Gene Deszca and Maurice Mazerolle, 'A Hitchhiker's Guide to Job Security: The Portfolio Career as a Response to Job Market Chaos.' **http://info.wlu.ca/~wwwsbe/faculty/tcawsey/career.htm**
85 Barrie Hopson and Mike Scally, *Build Your Own Rainbow: A Workbook for Career and Life Management* (Management Books, 2000).
86 *The Luck Factor* (Miramax, 2003).
87 Professor Tom Kirkwood, Director of CISBAN, Newcastle University in an address to The Foundation for Science and Technology on 'Raising Skills in the UK Workforce', 1st April 2009.
88 *The Element: How Finding Your Passion Changes Everything* (Allen Lane, 2009).
89 Carmine Gallo, *Fire Them Up!* (Wiley, 2007).

Step 8

My story

'A fact is like a sack – it won't stand up if it's empty. To make it stand up, first you have to put in it all the reasons and feelings that caused it in the first place.' Luigi Pirandello

Why tell stories?

Facts tell us, well, just the facts. They don't provide context, emotion or meaning. Which is a challenge for us humans because we're essentially emotional beings. We like to think we're incredibly rational but we make decisions very largely based on our feelings with the facts backing up that decision. Stories are a weaving of facts into a narrative that people find compelling and memorable. Stories help to tell people who we are. They help people feel they know us. They open us up and help to convey a sense of honesty and trust. And if people trust us and we make them feel good, they might just buy our services. As Pirandello says, you need reasons and feelings to make your story 'sack' stand up. And much like the sack, when we tell a good story, we go from being one dimensional to being three dimensional and infinitely more memorable.

The main question here is how can you help listeners to be interested in and remember you long after you've left? If listeners were to recall you and your story a week later, what do you think they'd say about you? If listeners were asked to give three words that describe you, based purely on your story, what would they say?

'A good story helps you influence the interpretation people give to facts. Facts aren't influential until they mean something to someone. A story delivers a context so that your facts slide into new slots in your listeners' brains.' Annette Simmons[90]

Daniel Pink in *A Whole New Mind*[91] writes:

'When facts become so widely available and instantly accessible, each one becomes less valuable. What begins to matter more is the ability to place these facts in context and to deliver them with emotional impact.'

There are many different types of stories including the corporate story, the industry story, the political story (these can be very memorable) but here we want to focus on *your* story.

A good story...
1 ...is all about connection and engagement.

If the first thing to understand about communication is that we're all selling something, then the second and even more crucial thing to understand is this:

'People buy on emotion and justify with fact.' Bert Decker[92]

Facts are important, but in and of themselves they don't really tell us very much. They certainly don't tell us about being human. One City business leader we spoke to said:

'I look at loads of fantastic CVs and on paper these people look great. But when it comes to interview time, they can't seem to pull these factual achievements into an interesting story. I don't care if one of their hobbies is kayaking – do they have a kayaking story that might actually tell me something about their character and personality?'

2 …helps the listener to reinterpret the facts. For example, you might be an accountant and could talk about yourself in this way:

'I qualified as an accountant aged 24. Over 14 years, I've worked for two large organisations. I worked for XYZ for seven years and ABC for five years. The last two years I've worked for the NSPCC.'

The amount of numbers and facts just plays to the stereotypical image of a boring accountant. Or you could choose to say:

'I work for the charity NSPCC, making sure as much of the money as possible goes to helping vulnerable children. I was an accountant for large organisations for 12 years. But after a friend persuaded me to man the donation telephone lines, where I had to talk to the public about the great work the charity does, I had a "lightbulb moment". I

could still be an accountant but for an organisation which fitted my values. Within a year, I'd changed jobs. I now love what I do and feel like I'm making a difference.'

Which person would you remember?

3 ...doesn't have to be long. Short is good.

'I made this letter longer than usual because I lack the time to make it shorter.' Blaise Pascal, *Provincial Letters XVI* (1660)

It's easy for many of us to ramble on about ourselves for a long time. Sometimes, a very l–o–n–g time. Indeed, we'd go as far as saying that most people's favourite subject is themselves. But in today's hyperconnected world, the winners are the people who can turn their 60-minute lecture into a 60-second YouTube clip, an interesting 20-second answer to 'And what do you do?' and a five-second tagline on their business card, website and e-mail signature.

Katie's story
'Katie went to Hong Kong in 1990' is a fact. But so what? Why is she telling us this? Well if she were trying to convey a sense of independence, adventure and ability to adapt, she might try this:

'Moving to Hong Kong in 1990 was a defining moment in my life. Due to a rather bad relationship situation, I followed an opportunity to work in HK knowing I couldn't return to the UK for at least a year. I knew no one. Starting as a personal trainer, I

- *reinvented myself part-time into a TV reporter by polishing my CV as brightly as possible.*

- *had breakfast with Richard Branson.*
- *created a portfolio career, which included voice-overs for kung fu movies, in-flight movie reviews for Cathay Pacific and playing Macbeth in an all-female theatre group.*
- *learned that anything was possible as long as you wanted it enough and worked for it. They were four great years, sometimes succeeding and sometimes failing. Basically, I figured out what I really wanted to do.*
- *Oh – and I met my future husband.'*

There's more context here. More 'reasons and feelings' for the listener to chew on. There are lots of mini-stories to follow up if they're interested or curious – but not too much to bore them witless. When we tell our stories, we need to think about what we really want to convey to the other party, especially when we're telling personal stories. It's all too easy to get carried away with the detail that we think is wonderfully exciting. But stop and look into the eyes of the other person. What do they tell you? Are they positively engaged or looking to move on? Do they ask for more detail or change the subject completely? Telling a story is all about connecting emotionally.

For example, in a job interview, once certain minimum criteria are fulfilled, what are the interviewers looking for? If they're convinced you can actually do the job, then they're looking for something more. Are you the sort of person who'll get along with the existing staff? Are you potential leadership material? Do they just get this feeling that even if you don't have exactly the required qualifications or experience, you're someone to be trusted? Someone who'll bring a certain energy to the job?

What we're talking about here are emotions. They're very powerful and we rely on them much more than we acknowledge. As mentioned above, the power of a story is that it can take us from being one dimensional to three dimensional. And it doesn't have to take very long.

'When you tell a story you invoke a power that's greater than the sum of the facts you report. It has emotional content and delivers a contextual framework and a wisdom that reaches past logical rational analysis.' Annette Simmons[93]

Katie used to be a TV news reporter and a presenter for ITN (5 News) and BBC. What all news organisations do is tell short stories. Usually, they tell them three times in one news programme:

1 Headline – 5 seconds.
2 Lead-in – 15 seconds (presenter in vision).
3 Report – 60 to 90 seconds.

Having reinvented herself with a portfolio communications career, this is how Katie now uses these principles:

(Headline) *'I help individuals and businesses to tell their stories with impact.'*

(Lead-in) *'I help individuals and businesses to tell their stories by creating impactful presentations and sales pitches, hosting and producing conferences, presentation coaching and writing a portfolio career blog and book.'*

(Report) *'I help individuals and businesses to tell their stories by creating impactful presentations and sales pitches, hosting and producing conferences, presentation coaching and writing a portfolio career blog. As a former TV news reporter, I feel everybody has a story to tell. My most powerful interviews have been with people who've been passionate about a 'cause'. That got me thinking about how I could help business people to tell their stories. Stories are an* *incredibly memorable way not only to get your key messages across but also to tell the audience a little about yourself.*

I help people to clarify messages, bring these to life and be themselves when communicating with different audiences. For example, recently I interviewed Steve Ballmer, CEO of Microsoft, in front of 350 people in London; I introduced Gordon Brown at an Innovation Event; I helped technical IT people in Moscow and Warsaw to communicate more effectively and created a memorable story helping to market a new online loan site.

I'm fascinated by how people use technology to improve their own and other people's lives. So I report for BBC 'Click' and other programmes that spread this message around the world. That led me to work with some large companies (Microsoft, Sony and 3). The Web is bringing people together like never before. Age, race, wealth, gender – there are very few barriers to entry. Which is why I started writing (with Barrie Hopson) a portfolio career blog. We've written a book on 10 steps to creating a portfolio career. We want to show people there is another way to find fulfilment in your work.'

CAN DO: Create your story

This is one of the most challenging exercises in the book but we believe it's one of the most important that you'll do, whether or not you've a portfolio career. Your ability to do this well will have a direct effect on how successful you'll be and consequently on how much money you'll earn.

Just the facts

Start with the first job in your portfolio or the one job you currently have. Using bullet points, list what roles you performed within that job. For example, one of the jobs in your portfolio may be that of teacher. So your list could look like this:

- 12 months – classroom assistant;
- 12 months – part-time classroom assistant plus two days study;
- 30 months – part-time qualified teacher for dyslexic children.

Go to your second job and repeat. Then your third job and so on. If you've only one job at the moment, list the roles you currently perform and then go back to your previous job and the job before that and list those.

1 Facts to stories

You'll now have two or more lists of facts about the jobs you currently do or have previously done. Look at the lists again. Take yourself back to that time and place. Ask yourself to recall the most interesting stories from that job. (It may also help to review your achievements from Step 3.) Think about stories that are:

- humorous;
- impressive (numbers, results, honours, articles);
- human;
- connected with someone famous or with a big name organisation/company.

Think how your story is memorable to someone who doesn't know you. For example, was there a specific event or incident that made you want to be a teacher? Did you read something? Did you meet someone who inspired you to do this work? Do you know someone or is there someone in your family who has done this? Ask friends or colleagues to recall why they believe you do what you do and why you decided to pursue this work. Ask them to share any stories they remember about you and this job. The important element is to think how these stories come across to another person. What will they be thinking about you as a result of hearing your stories? This should help you with the next part...

2 Choose two or three stories

You'll hopefully now have two or three stories about each of the jobs in your portfolio or in your current and previous jobs. But first, ask yourself:

'How will people remember me? How can I make it easy for them to talk about me in one or two sentences or better still, one or two words? How can I make it so memorable they'll be able to remember and talk about me in two weeks' time?'

The answer is in the story structure and how you deliver it. For example, two stories that could come from being a teacher of dyslexic children might be:

- **(Story 1)** I was inspired by my son's struggle. I wanted to help him keep up with the rest of the class. I could see it was badly affecting his school work but also his social relationships.
- **(Story 2)** Many successful people are dyslexic: Richard Branson is and he left school at 15. He sees dyslexia as positive; he had to simplify things to help himself and that also helped others. Other high-profile dyslexics are Olympic gold medallist rower Steve Redgrave and TV chef Jamie Oliver.

3 Combine these two or three stories into a narrative.

For example:

- **(What I am)** I'm a primary school teacher working specifically with children diagnosed as dyslexic.

- **(Story 1)** After my son was diagnosed as dyslexic, he worked with a special teacher who helped him to work on his spelling and reading. The difference in him in 12 months was amazing and best of all his confidence was building again. I was working as a teaching assistant at the time and decided to train to help children just like my son. The training was harder than I thought and I struggled to get through the qualification but finally completed it last summer, having met an inspiring lady who developed many of the techniques we now use.

- **(Story 2)** People think dyslexia is a real barrier to learning and being successful but many entrepreneurs like Richard Branson, for example, are dyslexic and he says it helped him to simplify things. Also the Olympic rower Steve Redgrave, TV chef Jamie Oliver and even Einstein were all dyslexic. It doesn't mean it's a barrier to success.

So here you have the story of what you do, why you do it, the family connection, personal challenge, personal success and identification with role models.

4 Less is more

'It was a speech about everything and therefore about nothing.' The Washington Post review of Bill Clinton's State of the Union address[94] in 1995.

Look again at your story. Remember the 15-second lead-in and the 60-second report we talked about earlier? Can you now shape and develop your story from the 60-ish seconds above to tell a similar story in 15 seconds? It could sound something like this:

'I'm a primary school teacher working with children diagnosed as dyslexic. My son's dyslexic and he's worked with a special teacher who helped with his spelling and reading. The results were amazing. From that, I decided to train to help children just like my son.'

This is short and sweet. It lets people know what you do and why you do it, family connection and personal challenge. It's also phrased in such a way as to entice the listener to ask more questions. It's a great way to open a conversation at an event, networking lunch or when you've just been introduced casually. You could also use this to explain more about yourself on your blog, website, social network or any printed materials (see Step 9: My brand).

5 Test it out

Try rehearsing your story. If your computer has a webcam, film and time yourself. Your digital camera may shoot video also. Set it up and do it. Keep talking to the camera just as if it were a person you're talking to. Imagine a scenario at an event, conference, informal interview or dinner where you'll be introduced to a few people in quick succession.

We like to use a Flip Video camera, which is so easy to use, to interview people for our blog and no – we don't get a fee for recommending it. If all else fails, many computers and smartphones have audio recording functions. Some colleagues have told us they feel embarrassed listening or watching themselves.Imagine how much more embarrassing it is if you mess up for real because of lack of practice.

You need to practise and see what works for you.

After suitable rehearsals, it's on to networking events. These are great places to try out your stories. Even if you hate (especially if you hate) networking face to face, this exercise should at least give you something to start the conversation. Try to stick to your story script for the first two or three people and then, depending on the reaction you get, think about whether or how you should modify it. Make notes on the reactions you get and try to 'take the best'. You could always ask the people you're talking to for their advice. What resonated best for them about your story? As long as you're honest about what you're trying to achieve, people will be only too happy to help.

6 Repeat for each job

Repeat the exercise above for each of the jobs in your portfolio.

7 My portfolio story

You should now have two or three mini-stories plus the 15-second and 60-second stories for each of the jobs in your portfolio. Try to think of each of the mini-stories as sweets in a jar and each time you speak about yourself and what you do, you can simply create a 'pick 'n' mix' 15 seconds or 60 seconds depending on who you're talking to.

For example:

'I have a portfolio career. I'm a teacher of dyslexic children and I'm also a Pilates instructor. My son's dyslexic and he's worked with a special teacher who helped with his spelling and reading. The results were amazing. From that, I decided to train to help children just like my son. Also, I've been practising Pilates for five years – ever since I hurt my back after falling off my mountain bike. I had a great teacher who suggested I should train to teach others. I qualified last year and now help around 12 clients a week including the CEO of XYZ company.'

The above is what we'd call the 'big picture story'. In this, you're communicating the big picture of all the offerings in your portfolio. While this may be what you're trying to convey, many people with portfolio careers tell us they first find out a bit about the other person and then tailor their story – usually focusing on the jobs or talents most relevant to their audience.

It takes a bit more working out to begin with but it also means you're not always communicating exactly the same story. The process doesn't become stale and repetitive. And the added bonus is that you really *do* have to listen to the other person!

CAN DO: Creating your stories

Using all the material you've created, you should be in a position to fill in a table like the one below. The table will help you practice telling any number of different stories – whether you just want to focus on one specific job in your portfolio or talk about any combination thereof.

	Job 1: school teacher	Job 2: Pilates instructor	Portfolio story
5-second headline	I help children to achieve their academic potential.	I help adults to achieve their physical potential.	'I help children and adults to achieve their academic and physical potential.
15-second lead-in	See point 4		See point 7
60-second report	See point 3		

Practise, practise, practise

What can you say in the first five seconds that will grab the listeners' attention and make them want to listen to more? For example in the story above, a first sentence or tagline could be:

'I help children to achieve their academic potential.'

That sounds like it's worth hearing more about, rather than, 'I'm a teacher'.

Think about your audience

What do they need to know? This isn't the same as what you want to tell them. Sometimes they can be vastly different stories. What's the context in which you're talking? Is it an interview, a networking event or a company event?

What parts of your story are most relevant to your audience?

Think about when others have introduced themselves to you. What, if anything, do you remember about them? And why? It could be that you remember them as being rather dull and to be avoided at all costs. Or that they sounded fascinating and that you really wanted to get to know them and their stories a bit better.

What we do know is that enthusiasm and energy delivered with credibility is infectious and if it's genuine, people react well and are prepared to listen just a little longer.

Delivery

Go back to the video. When you review your performance, don't listen just to the words. They're important, yes, but equally important is what you're saying in a non-verbal form. What's your face saying? We've all seen politicians deliver perfect oratory but at the same time we look at them and don't believe a word of it. Why? Because many are not authentic. The words and the body language don't match.

As humans, we know people can be taught to say all the right words but it's a lot more difficult for our faces and bodies to lie. And if we as listeners have to choose what to believe, we usually go with the non-verbal language and ask questions about whether we should trust these individuals and what they're saying.

Allan Pease, author of *The Definitive Book of Body Language*, believes women are far more perceptive than men. He points to an experiment by psychologists at Harvard University.

'They showed short films, with the sound turned off, of a man and woman communicating. The participants were asked to decode what was happening by reading the couple's expressions. The research showed women read the situation accurately 87 per cent of the time, while the men scored only 42 per cent. Men in 'nurturing' occupations such as artistic types, acting and nursing, did nearly as well as the women; gay men also scored well.'[95]

Storytelling makes you more confident

Think back to Step 3: My motivated skills, where we looked at your stories of achievement. Recent research[96] has shown that the value in this exercise isn't just limited to discovering your motivated skills. Indeed, a major discovery was the extent to which the participants found the apparently simple act of telling their stories of achievements to be a learning event in itself. One person noted:

'There is power in describing examples from the past to support a strength. I love to tell my story.'

In the process of telling their stories to others, people 'make conscious and explicit that which already exists implicitly, generally outside of your everyday awareness'.[97] McAdams confirms that, in his experience, people find the process 'profoundly enlightening'. He suggests it gets people thinking in ways they never would otherwise and in that process, they learn a lot about themselves.

The story exercise in this chapter is mainly focused on the listener impact – what we choose to say to someone else to get them to 'buy' us and our goods and services. In addition, we also know that 'telling stories of achievements appears to generate positive emotions'.[98]

So the actual process of uncovering what we did well helps to make us more confident. We just need to choose to dig a little into our memory banks and focus for a while on the many positives, on all those times we excelled and gave a bit extra. When we recall our successes instead of failures, we're not only able to communicate our stories better, but we make ourselves feel good too.

'To be a person is to have a story to tell.' Karen von Blixen

Summary
You've learned:

- why stories are good.
- the elements of a good story.
- how to engage, be brief and deliver with impact.
- how to create your 5-, 15- and 60-second 'one job' stories.
- how to create your 5-, 15- and 60-second 'portfolio' stories.
- how to think like your audience.
- how storytelling makes you more confident.

Notes

90 *The Story Factor* (Basic Books, 2006).

91 *A Whole New Mind* (Marshall Cavendish, 2008).

92 *You've Got to be Believed to Be Heard* (revised edition, St Martin's Press, 2008).

93 *The Story Factor* (Basic Books, 2006).

94 From Jerry Weissman's *Presenting to Win: The Art of Telling Your Story* (FT Press, 2003). **http://tinyurl.com/crvr2x**.

95 *The Definitive Book of Body Language* (Orion Books, 2005).

96 David Pilbeam, unpublished MA dissertation, 'How can coaching help people discover the patterns of their achievements and aid career development?', Oxford Brookes University, 2008.

97 D. P. Adams, *The Stories We Live By: Personal Myths and the Making of the Self* (The Guildford Press, 1993).

98 See footnote 96.

Step 9

My brand

'We are CEOs of our own companies: Me Inc. To be in
business today, our most important job is to be head marketer
for the brand called You. It's that simple – and that hard.'
Tom Peters[99]

CEO of Me Inc.

Jamie Oliver is a brand. Oprah is a brand. McDonald's is a brand.
And before starting a portfolio career, you need to think like one, too. A
brand is a trust mark, an authentic individual or organisation we can rely
on to deliver what we need, on time, on budget, with excellent service
and hopefully a little X factor. Think of a few brands you trust. Why do
you trust them? What have they consistently done to earn it? If they did

or said something inauthentic, how long would you trust them for? Ditto an individual brand. The disappointment factor is likely to be larger because you're much more closely integrated with the brand.

It takes a long time to build a great brand but can take seconds to destroy. An old saying goes: 'Confidence grows at the rate a coconut tree grows but falls at the rate a coconut falls'.

This applies to brands, too. You can spend a long period of time building up your reputation/brand and yet it can be compromised in a moment. In 2009, Michael Phelps, the amazing American Olympic swimmer and a US national hero, was suspended from competition for three months after photos were published appearing to show him smoking cannabis. He apologised for his 'regrettable behaviour' but didn't say whether he'd taken drugs. USA Swimming cut off its financial support to Phelps for the same three months and Kellogg's cereal company said, 'Michael's most recent behaviour is not consistent with our image and we have decided not to extend his contract.' The deal was reported to be worth £750,000. How long will it take him to rebuild his brand? How long before he regains public trust and that of his sponsors?

Brands are important to everyone, whatever career pattern you have. If you've developed a particular brand in a single-track career, for example, Ms Reliability in your department, and you suddenly let a customer down very badly, that trust/brand will have to be built up again. It might withstand one lapse but you'd better make sure it doesn't happen again. For portfolio workers, who may have more than one brand, it's just as crucial. In 1997, Fast Company[100] devoted a large section of its September edition to:

'The Brand Called You. You Can't Move Up If You Don't Stand Out!'

Some people, mostly IT professionals, artists and consultants, started to think and act differently. They began a journey of turning themselves into what's been termed Global Microbrands. Hugh MacLeod describes this as a small brand that 'sells' all over the world.

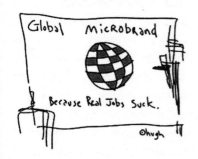

He says: 'The Global Micro-brand is nothing new; they've existed for a while, long before the Internet was invented. Imagine a well-known author or painter, selling his work all over the world. Or a small whisky distillery in Scotland. Or a small cheese maker in rural France, whose produce is exported to Paris, London, Tokyo etc. Ditto with a violin maker in Italy. A classical guitar maker in Spain. Or a small English firm making $50,000 shotguns.'[101]

This worked for some people with niche, high-quality products and services that spread by word of mouth. And with the Internet still largely one way – 'pushing' information instead of being a two-way interactive process – many people were still to be convinced…However, not one but two major global shifts have taken place since the late 90s.

World recession

'Arguably the global economic crisis will turn out to be more significant for us and other developed economies than the collapse of communism. A New Capitalism is likely to emerge from the rubble… This, in itself, is no reason for gloom or despair. For many, the New Capitalism may well seem fairer and less alienating than the model of the past 30 years, in that the system's salvation may require it to be kinder, gentler, less divisive, less of a casino in which the winner takes all.' Robert Peston[102]

This recession is obviously not just a small market 'correction'. Every country in the world has now felt the impact and is busily trying to get out of the mess. Will it take a year? Two years? Who knows? The brutal truth is that no one knows and anyone who says they do is kidding themselves. We do know one thing though. When the economy does bounce back, it won't be the same as before. The rules are changing… and that's not necessarily bad.

Recruitment company Hays,which cut 500 jobs at the end of 2008 said, 'The market is tough and will get tougher'. However, Hays went on to explain that temporary recruitment had grown by four per cent in the last quarter of 2008 as employers turned to short-term workers.[103]

Whatever your current work status, we would very strongly urge you to think like a freelancer[104]. If you knew your job was being axed in two months' time, what exactly would you be doing today, tomorrow and the day after that? If you knew you'd be searching for a new job or jobs, how would you go about it? Where would you start?

One of our favourite bloggers, Guy Kawasaki, says entrepreneurs shouldn't fear the financial crisis now. 'It doesn't matter whether the Dow is 5,000 or 50,000,' Kawasaki says. 'If you're an entrepreneur, there is no bad time to start a company. Entrepreneurs used to need millions of dollars to launch start-ups. Now, many get started with online tools from free software to affordable Web-hosting and blogging services.'[105]

Obviously, we'd suggest studying the first few Steps of this book as a starting point. Understanding my money, My motivated skills, My values and My 'selves' will help you to define what areas you want to explore. You can then use My networks, My portfolio, My story and this step, My brand, to develop it further. If Madonna can do it, so can you. Reinvention, we mean!

Web 2.0 – the Web changes everything

This is not media spin, hype or just mouthing off. We are living through nothing short of a revolution. The genuinely democratic, interactive, affordable, mobile, Web is here and growing rapidly. Changing what is possible and opening up opportunities for everyone.

And it's not just about the technology. Yes, it's there in the background as an enabler, but its powerful effect can be life changing. It revolutionises the way we earn, learn and turn round our careers. The authors of *Groundswell*[106] suggest it's a whole new way of interacting and communicating:

'The groundswell is a social trend in which people use technologies to get the things they need from each other instead of from companies.'

For example, Katie works for a number of large companies but usually is engaged to work by a few specific individuals, not a central purchasing hub. She can work on a project within a global company because she has the technology to do so. Anyone with a decent broadband connection and a half-decent computer can do the same. The people inside the large company want a job done well, to their specifications, on time and on budget. They get their desired project – Katie gets paid and gets to work with some talented people. It's a win–win situation.

Barrie shares presentations online with people who can't attend in person. He now updates his latest book on the 50+ population[107] via a blog, whereas in the past he would have to hope that enough books of the first edition were sold to enable a reprint and an updated second edition. We're doing the same with this book.

Large parts of the world can now communicate with each other virtually, free of charge, by using e-mail, blogs, Twitter, Instant Messaging, via text and video. We have instant access to the world's libraries. We can search for information on any product, service, company or individual in fractions of a second. And most importantly, online, you get to play with the big boys and girls. You have a chance to offer a better, more valuable niche service than many of the established players. You get to define your brand.

'Google me' is the new business card, and thus, the blog and social network profile is the new résumé.' Jeremiah Owyang, senior analyst, Forrester Research

Have you typed your name into Google lately? Go ahead, try it. What do you see? Do you get a mention? If someone you met at a business or social event just remembered your name and typed it in, what impression of you would they instantly get? And don't tell us you've never done this with anyone you've met. It's compelling. What trail do they leave? What little article, video or detail can we remember so we can start the next conversation?

Dig a little deeper into Facebook. What can we tell from a photo, their friends, what they talk about, their postings, family photos, how many virtual custard pies have they thrown? Click on that link to their blog. What are they really turned on by? What can they talk about knowledgeably for pages and pages? Maybe click on a video they've made. Oh, and they use Twitter?[108] Might be interesting to see what they tweet about and who's important to them.

Then go back and read their profile on a business social network like LinkedIn. Does it all tie together? Does it seem like the same person? Does it all feel consistent? Does it feel authentic? You can tell the people who 'get it'. The story is the same. It flows.

Welcome to your new CV

With the new interactive Web in today's hyper-connected world, you and your brand are never more than several clicks away. Essentially, the Web works because we're human. Yes it's built on bits and bytes, but it's primarily people powered and getting more so by the day. And guess what? As humans we have an insatiable appetite to communicate, share and create relationships with other people.

Your website...

...is an online place where you can bring together information, documents, photos and video examples of work and testimonials. It's like a shop front for you and your brand. Today, creating a website is pretty easy and cheap. Two of the most popular and free sites to help you do this are:

• Google Sites: **www.google.com/sites/help/intl/en/overview. htm**
• Microsoft Office Live: **www.officelive.com/free-website**

Both of these offer short videos explaining step by step what you need to do to get set up, plus some tips on how to maximise your website's impact. This process can take literally minutes or hours depending on how much info you add and how much you feel you need to highlight. Here's a (non-exhaustive) list of what you might like to include:

• title – maybe your 5-second story, e.g. 'Getting you heard';
• your 15 second story – maybe with a link to your 60-second story;
• professional-looking photo (not the drunken one on Facebook);
• examples of your work (written, photos, videos etc.);
• articles you've written (to help people understand the benefit of hiring you);
• articles from others (interesting to your readers);
• news updates (who you've worked for lately and what you did);
• customer testimonials;
• link to video or audio of you;
• photos of work-related stuff (e.g. accepting a prize for great work).

Think: what do your customers need to know about you and your work?

Not what do you want to say to your customers. Think about it. Sometimes these two can be very different. Try to see things from a customer perspective. If you went to a site, what would grab you? What would make you want to click through a few pages and find out more?

Remember that having a portfolio career means you're selling yourself: your key skills, abilities, talents and experience. But it also means you're selling the human you. And by that, we mean try to create a site that reflects the 'you' that you want people to see. It doesn't mean giving a false impression, but just the very best that you can be. With that in mind, here are a few tips.

- Keep the design clean, simple and easy to navigate.
- Avoid pop-ups and music.
- Make sure the home page instantly explains what you do and the benefits of working with you.
- Include examples of your work, videos and podcasts.
- Incorporate your blog.
- Provide links to other sites.
- Keep it human and warm.
- Give stuff away – articles, advice, links, reviews and DVDs.

Finally, get a few people you trust to try out your site and ask them for constructive feedback so that you can make it even better.

It's good to blog

'There are thousands of reasons why people write blogs. But it seems to me the biggest reason that drives the bloggers I read the most is, we're all looking for our own personal global microbrand. That is the prize. That is the ticket off the treadmill. And I don't think it's a bad one to aim for.' Hugh MacLeod

Using the website as your 'shop front' analogy, it should be beautifully designed in such a way as to lure people in. But the challenge with a static website is that it *is* rather like a shop front – you can look but you can't touch. You can't interact with a stand-alone website and it rarely updates itself. So, if your website is your shop front, then your blog is your café.

What is a blog?

A Web log – aka a blog – is a sort of online diary. It has entries called posts, with the latest one always at the top, and can have text, photos and videos. The great thing about a blog is that people can subscribe to it via e-mail or a blog reader[109] and leave comments to either start or join in the conversation.

By using free and simple software, you can instantly publish your thoughts, ideas and comments to the world. So your blog is also another outlet for you to showcase your talents and passions. A CV can tell so much but it's generally a collection of facts in chronological order. A blog allows you to enthuse about topics you (and hopefully your customers) find exciting.

A blog is also a search engine magnet. All the big search services love content that updates regularly. It's even better if your blog has numerous links from and to it.

In March 2009, there were an estimated 210 million[110] blogs worldwide. So someone must think it's a good idea. There are some great ones (and let's be honest, plenty of rubbish ones, too) about news, sport, entertainment, finance, travel, etc., by all the big corporations. But it's often the personal and social ones that offer the richest rewards in terms of connections.

Why read blogs?
From a blog you can:

- learn something new and join the conversation;
- make friends with people who share your passions and interests;
- help others to succeed;
- help yourself to succeed.

'The word "blog" is irrelevant; what's important is that it is now common, and it will soon be expected that every intelligent person (and quite a few unintelligent ones) will have a media platform where they share what they care about with the world.'
Seth Godin (US business author, speaker and blogger)[111]

How to find great blogs
Before deciding whether blogging is for you, just go and read some. We don't suggest all 210 million but maybe start your search at **www.blogsearch.google.com**, **www.technorati.com** or the coolest, **www.icerocket.com**. These sites work off 'tags', which are labels that the authors put on their blog posts to make it easier for the blog search engines to find them. So you may go to technorati and type in 'portfolio

careers' and will get just over 700 blog posts all about portfolio careers. If you go to **blogsearch.google** the same search term delivers more than 1,879,000 posts, while icerocket delivers just over 2,500 posts.

Try them all. You'll soon find which work best for you. Depending on the number and the relevance of their results, you can then keep refining until you get closer to what you're looking for.

Another great source is **www.Alltop.com** created by branding hero, Guy Kawasaki.[112] His personal site is worth a visit just as an example of how to keep the shop-front clean and simple and use it to link to the blog. Alltop is what's called an 'aggregator site' and has categories such as work, health, culture, interests, technology, people, news, geography and sports. For example, let's say you're interested in careers advice. So go to the site, click on 'work' and then 'careers' and at least five of the most popular blogs will show along with the last five posts on each of them. These get updated every 15 minutes or so. That's also where you'll now find our blog.

You can also read the blog of someone you respect and admire and take a look at their 'blogroll': yes, it really is a word. This is a list of blogs they're reading and recommending to others.

By finding interesting and informative blogs and leaving constructive comments, you can start to build relationships with people who're at the top of their game and, usually as a by-product, they know a lot of interesting people. By commenting on people's blogs, it makes you want to meet that person face to face. It means you instantly have something to talk about and you feel as if you know quite a bit about that person already. They usually post a photo, which helps a great deal when trying to picture that person in your head.

Blog alert

Another way to find blog posts that may be of interest is to set up e-mail alerts (**www.google.com/alerts**) regarding any topic you're interested in. This will then e-mail you with any recent posts that mention the topic you've requested. It's a great way to see who's writing about the areas you care about and also to see who they're linking to.

Blogging has many benefits but doesn't replace the act of meeting face to face. What it does give us is information about the person whose blog we're reading and links to more fascinating content. It also makes connecting in person a lot easier because we already know a lot of the basics about that person and can quickly go into the areas of mutual interest.

Got something to say?

Then blog it.

www.blogger.com is one of the simplest, free blogging sites and comes with a short, handy video to explain exactly how to set it up – **http://www.youtube.com/BloggerHelp.**

You could also try one of the most popular: **http://wordpress.com.**

Microsoft is in the game with a combination of a blog and social networking tool in the shape of spaces: **http://tinyurl.com/cuoras.**

Just imagine, in somewhere between 15 minutes and 15 hours, you can be up and publishing to the world.

Computer manufacturer, Dell[113], has embraced the social media world and now is on Facebook offering advice to small businesses on how to get the best out of it. There are many guides including:

Part 1: Learn to Listen
Part 2: Join the Conversation
Part 3: Start a Blog
Part 4: Tap into Twitter
Part 5: Crowdsource Your Next Big Idea
Part 6: Harness the Power of Facebook
Part 7: Share Photos and Videos Online
Part 8: Measure Your Success Online

What do I write?

Having read a few blogs, you should now have a better understanding of what's interesting and informative and what engages you, as a reader. Here are some tips.

- Try to entertain, educate and engage your target audience. What do they want to know about?
- Take a different or specific industry angle on today's news.
- Keep it short.
- Include a picture, photo and/or short video.
- Write a catchy headline – think *The Sun* newspaper.
- Link to other interesting articles or blog posts.
- Think lists.
- Use tags.
- Be an expert in your chosen field.
- Respond to people who leave comments.
- Be patient.
- Post often – at least twice a week.[114]
- Have a blogroll.

Finally, don't forget to ask yourself, 'Is this interesting to my audience?'.

Blogtastic: some notable blogs

Hannah's Country Kitchen[115] – this is what she says on her blog:

'Reaching the final of Masterchef 2007 *was a rollercoaster of emotion, with huge highs and lows, but I loved every minute and learnt a huge amount. I owe a great deal to John and Gregg who had faith in my ability when I did not believe in myself. Since competing on the programme my life has changed considerably. I now write cookery columns for two magazines, give cookery demonstrations*

and am writing my second cook book. I love all forms of country cooking, using seasonal and locally sourced produce. This blog is to enable me to share with you a few of my recipes and baking ideas. Enjoy. Hannah xxxx'

Hannah Miles moved from a job in the City of London to the country where she could have a garden and a more relaxed quality of life with a short commute. She's an in-house (literally based in her own house) lawyer working across seven small companies, a professional cook, writer for cooking magazines and now an author of a book which she describes as 'cake heaven'.[116]

She says, 'This work style allows me to pursue a dream job – I can use my professional experience and at the same time have a feeler out to see what I can earn as a cook. It enables me see the value in what I have to offer. It's flexible. I can take an hour's break from my work to cook or do a photo shoot.'

The blog allows Hannah to keep in touch with her audience and quickly react to their feedback. If you are a secret cake lover, we strongly suggest you visit her blog. It's incredible what she can do with a Victoria sponge…

Steve Clayton – award-winning Geek in Disguise[117] – on his blog he says:

'I'm a technology geek at heart and use this blog to share stuff, introduce people I meet and generally talk about the impact software can have around the world. I make no apologies for when it goes off the rails:).'

Steve Clayton works for Microsoft and has done so for 12 years. He enjoys what he does enormously but knows that even working for a mega-successful IT company doesn't guarantee you a job for life.

'I started blogging because 1. I'm a frustrated journalist. 2. I wanted to increase the number of customers I could help. 3. Help to change the external perception of Microsoft and 4. Create a personal 'bookshelf' (keep everything I'm interested in in one place). I had a choice to make it purely a work blog or a 'Steve Clayton – the guy that works for Microsoft' blog. I chose the latter. I just say 'I blog about technology, social media, design, architecture and generally stuff I like and it turns out other people like the same stuff. My blog has become my living CV, my online brand…if I were thinking of leaving Microsoft, the first people I would approach would be those I met through my blog.'

So blogging and building your personal brand don't just start when you already have a portfolio career. They should start way before that and actually help to point you in directions you hadn't previously thought about, working for people you'd never considered.

Mike Pegg has a **Strengths Academy blog**.[118] The 3 Tips series offers a new practical tool for building on strengths each weekday. It's a way of getting his message to a number of interested individuals. He also has numerous other links to great strengths pioneers and creates short biographies. The great thing about the Web is that you may have fans of your work that you've never met and may never meet. It also builds your trust and credibility factor. This is a man who really is on a mission to help people succeed.

The Rubbish Blog[119] – this is what it says on the blog:
Can the average person really create zero waste? The challenge was set and during the week 10–17 March 2008, one mother in Bury St Edmunds gave it a go. She only threw out a plaster. Can you do it too? Why not try your own Rubbish Diet and slim your bin. You'll be

amazed at how easy it really is and you could even save some money. If Almost Mrs Average can do it, you can too.

'Almost Mrs Average', Karen Cannard says, 'I have slimmed my bin down to size 0 and am now inspiring others to reduce their waste'.

Karen is in the process of writing a book on this subject and regularly appears in print media and on radio.

Other blogs we rate

- Hugh McLeod – **www.gapingvoid.com**
- Seth Godin – **sethgodin.typepad.com**
- Tom Peters – **www.tompeters.com**
- Guy Kawasaki – **http://blog.guykawasaki.com**
- Garr Reynolds – **www.presentationzen.com**
- Daniel Pink– **www.danpink.com/**
- **www.Swiss-Miss.com** – great design ideas
- **www.Englishcut.com** – small bespoke tailor (comes out top Google search for Savile Row tailor)

How will they find you?

Tagging and 'pinging' to technorati[120] are important but the most important action is to leave comments on other people's blogs. It's like a snail leaving a trail. (Or trailing breadcrumbs, if snails don't work for you.) People reading your comment will be able to see where you're blogging from and will probably go and read your blog. They're always looking for new material to post and may well link from their blog to yours, thereby instantly sending their audience to you. There's a good reason it's called the Web.

Expert bloggers advise three strategies for your blog to be successful: link, link and link. Link to your previous posts, link to other people's posts and link to interesting sites or articles.

'*The act of writing a blog changes people, especially business people. The first thing it does is change posture. Once you realise that no one has to read your blog, that you can't make them read your blog, you approach writing with humility and view readers with gratitude. The second thing it does is force you to be clear. If you write something that's confusing or in shorthand, you fail. Respectful and clear. That's a lot to get out of something that doesn't take much time.*' Seth Godin[121]

How do I find out how many people are visiting my blog?

Sign up for a free tracking service. We use **www.statcounter.com** but **www.icerocket.com** also offers a tracking service. The instructions on how to add these to your blog are given on the sites and do demand some concentration. However, Barrie did this for his blog **www.theplusesofbeing50plus.blogspot.com** within 30 minutes of logging on to the statcounter site. (He's not a natural geek so anyone should be able to do it.)

We know from Forresters Technographics Surveys[122] that far more people read blogs than ever comment so don't get dispirited if you get few or even no comments to begin with. The Groundswell authors have a special website, **www.groundswell.forrester.com**, which you can access to get the latest data on who is doing what on blogs in a wide range of countries.

They distinguish between six types of social media users: alongside each you can see the user data for March 2009 in the UK for all ages and genders.

- **Creatives** – people who publish a blog, their own Web pages, upload videos, write articles and post them (15 per cent).

- **Critics** – those who review, comment on blogs and contribute to online forums (20 per cent).
- **Collectors** – people who use RSS feeds, use Google Alerts and add tags to web pages (5 per cent).
- **Joiners** – those who visit social networking sites and maintain their profiles on these sites (28 per cent).
- **Spectators** – people who read blogs, watch videos, listen to podcasts and read customer reviews (49 per cent).
- **Inactives** – those who do none of these (42 per cent).

To promote your brand you really should be a creator, failing that a critic, or at the very least a collector.

Log the blog

Without getting too geeky, if you want to read a few blogs every day it's best to subscribe to a blog reader – also called an RSS reader. Google reader[123] is a fine one. RSS stands for Really Simple Syndication and has a logo like this but in bright orange.

Once you've downloaded the free RSS reader software, you just go to a blog you want to subscribe to (usually free) and press the orange button. This will then show up in your reader. It's a bit like news headlines – so you can quickly read the first line before deciding whether to open the whole post. The great thing about it is that when a new post is created, it just automatically appears in your RSS reader. Your e-mail inbox isn't clogged up and when you want to add or delete blogs, it just takes a couple of clicks. It's a great way to stay informed and connected.

Using Twitter

Twitter[124] is a free micro-blogging service that allows people to send and read updates ('tweets') from others that are limited to 140 characters.

Tweets are usually public but you can tweet directly if you wish. Users receive updates via **http://twitter.com**, e-mail, Facebook, text, RSS or if you want to get a bit more techie, through specific applications.

This is how Twitter describes itself:

'Twitter is a service for friends, family, and co-workers to communicate and stay connected through the exchange of quick, frequent answers to one simple question: What are you doing?*'*

We admit it does sound quite strange to start with but once you've tried it, it can become rather addictive. And useful.

Why? The benefits of Twitter...

One person we spoke to described Twitter as a bit like, 'All my friends down the pub where I can always pop in to chat to them'.

Essentially, a lot has been written and spoken about Twitter but its benefits seem to fall into these three areas. It delivers:

1 Trust – it's a brilliant recommendation engine.
2 Speed – it's the fastest delivery system in the world.
3 Brand – it helps build your personal brand and network.

What do we mean by a 'recommendation engine'? The strength of Twitter is that it's an 'open' network. You don't have to ask people's permission to be able to 'follow' them but at the same time it offers users a private message facility as well as a public one. It's built on trust. You trust your community to help you with a question. You might be looking for a good value hotel to stay on holiday in New York – what would people recommend and why? You'll quickly have access to the 'wisdom of the crowd'[125]: essentially, the aggregation of information from many individuals, resulting in better decisions. Why do we trust these people? Maybe because we know in most cases, they don't have an agenda. Their lives won't be affected whether or not we act on their advice. We used to trust banks and large companies. Now we place more trust with our friends – real or virtual.

You might not think speed is important but as portfolio workers, we sometimes need to get work done quickly and efficiently. Instant access to the right individual with the ability to make a quick decision can be critical and make the difference between something being just 'good' and turning out 'great'.

Twitter has been compared with Facebook, especially with regard to its status updates. But Twitter users have pretty much ignored the 'what are you doing?' question and instead use it as kind of instant blog. It's a great way to get real-time feedback and it creates the feeling of eavesdropping on conversations and interesting links. Some bloggers suggest that using words such as 'how to', 'best', 'most', 'great', 'worst' and 'soon', will result in that tweet being clicked more often. It forces the writer to think of a short, snappy way to entice the reader. Not a bad thing.

Twitter shortens Web addresses, making it easy to share links to articles, websites, videos and photos – which help to build that brand. It can also be accessed via mobile phone.

'The new résumé is 140 characters.' tweets 23-year-old Amanda Mooney, who just landed a job in PR.[126]

Is this statement a tweet too far? We think she's got a point and 140 characters could be your 5-second story (see Step 8: My story) plus a link to your blog. Your blog, of course, will have numerous examples of your work, photos, videos, testimonials and most importantly, will say a whole lot more about you than a paper CV ever could. More than enough to get a potential employer to grant you an audience.

How?

Simple. Go to **http://twitter.com** and just put in a username, password and e-mail address. Now you're ready to go. Of course, you then find interesting people using Twitter's 'find people' or even better, see who your friends are following – you're bound to know some of them, the ones you don't may well have great information or insight. This 'Twitter in plain English' video[127] is brilliant. This 'Intro to Twitter' video[128] although a little longer tells you more about how small businesses can benefit, as does this document.[129]

Who?

Within minutes of asking what the three main benefits of using Twitter are, Katie received this from David Brain,[130] CEO of Edelman, Europe.

'Keeps you front of mind without being too intrusive/showcases your interesting life (or not)/serendipity happens!' from Web in reply to katieledger

'I love how Twitter confirms my all too often assaulted belief that humans are kind, curious, knowledgeable, tolerant and funny. The absurd constraints of the 140 character tweet seem oddly to bring out the best in wit, insight and observation.' Stephen Fry[131]

Celebrity users include Stephen Fry, Jonathan Ross, Barack Obama, Britney Spears and Andy Murray. Large companies such as Dell, Ford, Microsoft and Starbucks are getting in on the act too. And hundreds of thousands of portfolio workers looking to stay connected informed and open to their next opportunity. Give it a twirl...

Keeping up with technology

'If you want to know what is likely to happen in the future, the best advice is to ignore futurologists and talk to your children. Today's school-age children have been labelled by media commentators as 'the connected generation'. They have grown up with digital media and are masters of a world in which they will always be more comfortable than their parents'.[132] David Brain and Martin Thomas

Marketing my brand

Your personal brand is you. And everything you are, do and say. So be careful. Seth Godin on his blog quotes a cautionary tale relating to this.

'A friend advertised on Craigslist for a housekeeper. Three interesting résumés came to the top. She Googled each person's name.

The first search turned up a MySpace page. There was a picture of the applicant, drinking beer from a funnel. Under hobbies, the first entry was, 'binge drinking'.

The second search turned up a personal blog (a good one, actually). The most recent entry said something like, 'I am applying for some menial jobs that are below me, and I'm annoyed by it. I'll certainly quit the minute I sell a few paintings.'

And the third? There were only six matches, and the sixth was from the local police department, indicating that the applicant had been arrested for shoplifting two years earlier.

Three for three. Google never forgets.

Of course, you don't have to be a drunk, a thief or a bitter failure for this to backfire. Everything you do now ends up in your permanent record. The best plan is to overload Google with a long tail of good stuff and to always act as if you're on Candid Camera, because you are.'

Marketing your brand needn't be complicated if you're aware of the impact you're having on others. Every time you say something, send an e-mail, publish a blog post, tweet, meet someone, network and answer the phone, you're saying something about yourself. You may not think that, but in many cases the people we deal with have very little information about us. First impressions count. A lot.

As people in the customer service business like to say, 'You never get a second chance to make a first impression'. With that in mind, we offer up a list you might want to think about.

1 Appearance

Does it matter? Yes, it does. It matters to dress appropriately. If you don't know what that is, err on the side of caution and dress smartly. But make it your job to find out what is expected clothes-wise. You can always go nuts after they are so wowed by your work, by then they won't care.

Women, and we know this isn't fair, but please think about how low cut your top is and how high your skirt is. This is a new age but if women (and we have seen quite a few top-level execs) dress as if they're going clubbing, then women will never be really treated as equals.

Men, if you are on the weightier side, get some clothes that actually fit. You might think that baggy shirts are hiding the excess but they're actually making it look worse. Get a shirt that fits. Similarly, if you wear a suit, make sure it's the right size or consider getting one made. It could be a great investment in how you look and how it makes you feel.

Your hair. No matter how challenging times are, always make time and budget for a visit to the hairdresser's or barber's. Think about what image you want to project. Even if it's a bit 'different', do 'different' well. If you favour the 'unstructured' look, make sure your potential client doesn't think you just look a mess. And as a bonus, it's amazing what a new hairstyle can do for your self-esteem.

2 Promptness

Woody Allen said: 'The secret of my success is showing up.' [133]

He should have added 'on time'. For us this is a given. Why doesn't everyone do it?

'You can be or do whatever you want just by showing up. If you want to be an author, show up to write your manuscript every day, show up to writing classes, show up to phone calls to editors. Doesn't it make sense that someone who arrives at the door of opportunity has more success than someone just sitting at home? So increase your chances by 80 per cent. Show up!

3 E-mail signature

Think of your e-mail signature as an advertising hoarding. It's an opportunity to direct your reader to learn more about you and what you do. It should have your 5-second story or tagline and links to your website, blog and twitter account. You may want to think about different signatures for the different jobs you do. Or if all your jobs can be brought together, then one will be fine.

You might be more humorous with certain clients, but just make sure the tone of the mail is right. If you're not sure, don't send it immediately. Wait a few hours or overnight and look again. You'll have your answer. Also, if you've done a particularly great piece of work you want people to see, create a hyperlink to it in your e-mail signature. Don't leave it there too long and don't use it all the time but if you're really proud of it, use it.

4 Business cards

'I believe the effect will be less "applying" for jobs, more of employers finding you.' Libby Sartain, chief people officer, Yahoo!

@hugh

Dan Schawbel, author of *Me 2.0: Build a Powerful Brand to Achieve Career Success*[134] claims that already one in five hiring managers use social networks for background checks. So be very, very careful and check what the web has to reveal about you.

The rise of social networking and being 'virtually' introduced has reduced the requirement for these (and increased the need for a stunning e-mail signature). But when they're called upon, they'd better be good. The question here is whether you have a theme that runs through all your jobs and if you want to link them all together. We have spoken to people who have at least two cards. They like to keep the stories/jobs separate. Or you can just go for the bland personal details card. Think carefully if you include a photo of yourself – what does it say about you? It may be right if you're looking for customer facing work or you may feel it's a step too far. Katie has one of Hugh's cartoons on her business cards. This, despite her mother saying it's rude (it *is* slightly rude but it works for Katie). Whatever you put on there, make sure it's a reflection of your own personality. If in doubt, you could always have a 'safe' business card as well as a slightly 'wild' one – and offer them out as appropriate.[135]

Card checklist:

- name
- mobile number
- e-mail address
- website address
- blog address
- Twitter name
- address (maybe). This is an interesting one. Katie never uses her physical address because she has an office at home and thinks it can pay to appear bigger than you are. Of course, if you have a terribly impressive address then it could be a bonus but if not, it's something you have to think about. Some people don't put their address on their cards so that fact in itself can become a talking point and therefore memorable.

Make your card memorable. How will people remember you a week from now?

5 Give it away...information, expertise and advice

We've previously mentioned that the Web works best when people are giving and sharing. You never know who's watching or listening. If you get involved in the online communities that excite you, you'll receive more than you give. Rajesh Setty[136] has a long list of good advice on this one.

6 10-touch marketing campaign

Some years ago when Barrie was working with the Hay Group, he was impressed by the emphasis that they put on keeping in constant touch with their clients. All of their consultants were told to develop a 10-touch marketing campaign for each of their key clients. This meant reminding your client of your existence at least 10 times a year. In those days that mostly involved telephone calls, visits, lunch invitations to talk about new products or ideas (but not hard selling), sending birthday cards and Christmas cards, etc. These days, as we've said, it's much easier to do this by e-mailing articles, blog references, PowerPoint presentations, and soon. You don't have to individualise each e-mail but it certainly makes more of an impression when you do.

7 Mobile portfolio

If your work requires you to show clients some examples, e.g., if you're a decorator, chef, artist, general creative type, you could transfer some photos or short videos of your best work onto your mobile phone. It's the ultimate quick pitch to clients. 'Here's an example of what I love to do.' It works particularly well on an iPhone but any smart phone will do.

8 Offline versus online

Make sure the offline brand matches the online one. You don't want to offer something you can't deliver. Remember, your next project could come as a result of your last project. Why? Well you might be an expert in a particular field. You may be able to point someone towards a website, report, person or piece of information that could be useful to them. Expect nothing in return. But what you've done is plant a seed in that person's brain.

For example, the people we work for and the 'loose ties' in their networks now have a small 'Katie Ledger awareness' cell. This means that when they need some help with creating and communicating a message, presenting, event hosting then they know the person to contact. She will (hopefully) be at the top of that particular contact list. She may be the only person they think of – even better! For Barrie, hopefully, there will be a similar awareness cell when it comes to any issues regarding career development, lifeskills, customer service, the over 50s and, in particular, around older workers.

By sharing your knowledge and contacts, your network gets stronger. If you only remember one piece of advice from this book, please make it this one:

HELP OTHERS TO SUCCEED. YOU WILL TOO.

Remember Carol Stone's definition: *'Networking is making the most of the people you meet to your mutual advantage.'*

Finally...

Visualise a brand 'tree' (like Katie's hand-drawn version below). Think of yourself and your personal brand as a tree trunk made up of solid values and core strengths. These support and enhance your 'branches'– your different jobs or stories.

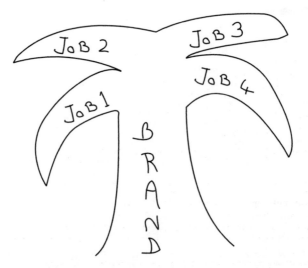

Think of Oprah Winfrey. Or just Oprah (when you're that famous you don't need a surname). Some of her branches are:

- TV host and producer
- author
- magazine publisher
- film director
- TV network owner
- retailer

And probably another dozen jobs that we haven't mentioned. She *is* the brand.

'We are all already, walking brands. We just have to polish them so that we can see them shine.'[137]

Time to start polishing...

Summary

- You are the brand.
- Recession plus Web 2.0 equals opportunity.
- Your new CV is online.
- Create a 'My Brand' website.
- Blog to build credibility and business.
- Twitter – give it a try...
- Marketing – everything you are, do and say.

Notes
99 www.fastcompany.com/magazine/10/brandyou.html
100 www.fastcompany.com
101 www.gapingvoid.com/Moveable_Type/archives/001976.html
102 Extract from analysis of the current crisis by Robert Peston on his BBC blog, Peston Picks, 8 December 2008.
103 www.telegraph.co.uk/finance/financetopics/recession/4174602/UK-jobs-market-is-getting-tougher-by-the-month-says-Hays.html
104 http://en.wikipedia.org/wiki/Freelancer
105 http://blog.guykawasaki.com

106 Charlene Li and Josh Bernoff, *Groundswell* (Harvard Business School Press, 2008).

107 **www.theplusesofbeing50plus.blogspot.com**

108 **http://twitter.com**

109 One of the popular ones can be found at **www.google.com/reader**

110 **www.technorati.com/blogging/state-of-the-blogosphere**

111 Seth Godin, *Tribes* (Penguin, 2008).

112 **www.guykawasaki.com/** You should also dip in and out of his book, *Reality Check: The Irreverent Guide to Outsmarting, Outmanaging, and Outmarking Your Competition* (Portfolio, 2009).

113 **www.facebook.com/dellsocialmedia**

114 We cannot overemphasise this. The technological consultants Gartner estimates that there are more than 200 million former bloggers who have ceased posting to their online diaries, creating an exponential rise in what has been described as 'dotsam' and 'netsam' – i.e. unwanted objects on the Web (analogous to flotsam and jetsam).

115 **http://hannahscountrykitchen.blogspot.com**

116 **http://tinyurl.com/cypm7x**

117 **http://blogs.msdn.com/stevecla01/**

118 **www.strengthsacademy.com/mikes-blog/**

119 **http://therubbishdiet.blogspot.com** – shortlisted for Media Guardian Innovation Awards - Independent Media category, 2009.

120 **http://support.technorati.com/support/siteguide**

121 **http://sethgodin.typepad.com/seths_blog/2007/02/if_no_one_reads.html**

122 Quoted in *Groundswell* by Charlene Li and Josh Bernoff (Harvard Business Press, 2008).

123 **www.reader.google.com**

124 **http://twitter.com**

125 James Surowiecki, *The Wisdom of Crowds: Why the Many Are Smarter Than the Few and How Collective Wisdom Shapes Business, Economies, Societies and Nations* (Little, Brown, 2005).

126 **http://tinyurl.com/5qywbd**

127 **http://tinyurl.com/c4vp2p**

128 **http://tinyurl.com/c89qzq**

129 **http://tinyurl.com/dhydcx**

130 **http://www.sixtysecondview.com/**

131 Quoted in *Telegraph Weekend*, Saturday 7 February 2009.

132 David Brain and Martin Thomas, *Crowd Surfing: Surviving and Thriving in the Age of Consumer Empowerment* (A & C Black, 2008).

133 **www.persistenceunlimited.com/2006/03/woody-allens-success-secret/**

134 *Me 2.0: Build a Powerful Brand to Achieve Career Success* (Caplan, 2009).

135 **www.streetcards.co.uk**

136 **http://tinyurl.com/aeztq3**

137 **Julie Anixter 29/12/08 blog post, www.tompeters.com**

Step 10

My portfolio career: Next steps

@hugh

Bringing it all together

You've now completed Steps 1 to 9 (or as many of them as you chose to) that we suggested could help you to create a portfolio career. Some of you will already have a portfolio career or have begun to develop one. These Steps, therefore, will hopefully have served as a checklist against which to assess your progress.

At this point it'll be useful to bring all of the data together. So let's review. How many of these questions can you answer for yourself now?

- Step 1: Is a portfolio career right for you?
- Step 2: How will you manage your finances?
- Step 3: What are your motivated skills?
- Step 4: What are your values?

- Step 5: What are your 'selves'?
- Step 6: Who is in your support network?
- Step 7: What is or will be in your portfolio?
- Step 8: What are your stories?
- Step 9: What is your brand?

We now need to look at some of the areas you might want to explore to help you live your portfolio career.

They are:

- Managing your future
- Managing your time and work
- Managing your energy
- Managing pressure and stress
- Managing transitions and change
- Learning from 'failures'
- The never-ending journey...learning and developing
- Learn to love new technology

Managing your future

Where do you want to be in five years? Each of us needs to spend some time thinking about the future. But this doesn't have to be prescriptive. Barrie constantly confounds people with his statement about his future that, 'I don't want to make definite plans. I like to plan my life so that I'm always open to spontaneity. As a specialist in career development, many people find that odd if not hypocritical. However, it's only as a result of going through the kind of career review that we write about in this book that I've been able to come to that view. One of my best friends worked out what he wanted to do with his career by the time he was 24. He's achieved it, by the way. Whereas my horror would be to be introduced to a fortune teller who really could foretell my future.'

People who are fortunate enough to an Apple computer will be familiar with a wonderful software program called Time Machine. (Katie would like to point out that she is a PC girl, which is why we make a good team.)

Time Machine backs up every hour or so but the beauty is that you can go back into its history and restore your computer exactly as it was an hour ago, a week ago, a month ago or a year or more ago.

CAN DO: Using your own 'time machine'

If you've worked your way through the steps outlined above, then you'll have created the total tapestry that is you as you are today. You know your motivated skills, your work values and the range of selves that make up the total you.

You've looked at how you manage your finances and your support networks. You've described the brand that summarises who you wish to project to others and the story lines that you use in describing yourself. You've also listed the job or jobs that you're doing and that you'd like to do. So now let's look at where you came from and where you might be going.

1 Restore yourself. Use your 'time machine' to go back five
   years. Write down the date: _____
2 Remind yourself of who you were then.

What were you doing? Who were you doing it with? Where were you living? What was important to you? How did you spend your time? What frustrations did you have? What plans did you have? Describe the real you that you've restored. Use the present tense i.e. 'I am doing this, etc.'

_____

_____

_____

_____

_____

3 Now back to the present. You've access to a very special, as yet uninvented time machine program – and even Barrie has to admit that this is something that his iMac can't do. **Create yourself** as you'd like to be five years from now. Write in the date that you're moving to: _____

Now describe yourself as the person you'd like to be by that date. Use the same questions that you used when you 'restored' yourself. But this time project yourself forward. Again, use the present tense as this makes the process more powerful.

_____

_____

_____

_____

4 How do you feel about the person you've created?

_____

_____

_____

_____

5 What will you need to do to create this person?

_____

_____

_____

_____

6 What will you need to stop doing to be able to create this person?

_____

_____

_____

_____

If a portfolio career is for you, read on!

The rest of this Step now looks at the issues that consistently came up when we interviewed people. They're also reflected in the research studies we reviewed. These are the particular challenges faced by portfolio workers followed by suggestions from them and from us as to how best to deal with them.

You'll need to able to manage:
- time and work flow;
- energy;
- pressure and stress;
- transitions and change;
- 'failure';
- to continue learning and developing;
- new technology.

Managing your time and work flow

Every portfolio worker talks about how vital it is to manage their complicated timetables.

'You need to be highly self-disciplined – but if you're not, you can train yourself.' Tanya Smith

One of the possible pluses of a portfolio career is that, in theory, you've greater control of when and how you work. This is important not just because of other life priorities but because as individuals our brains are wired in different ways. Many readers will know that they're 'owls' – people who work best later in the day and who like to stay up late and get up late. The 'larks', however, are the opposite, being at their most creative in the morning. One of the consequences of the Industrial Revolution which has continued to dominate our places of work and education was that everyone had to do the same thing at the same time.

Even today, many people have to report to a place of work irrespective of how their neural wiring will dictate their effectiveness.

About 10 per cent of individuals are classic larks and another 10 per cent are classic owls. The rest, who've been described as 'hummingbirds'[138], will approximate to one end of the scale or the other. Most people certainly have preferences but single-track and serial careers usually offer little flexibility no matter what kind of bird you are. Katie tends towards being a lark, which is just as well as she has two young children who get up early each morning…then at night she's had to talk creatively with a co-author who's an owl.

There are many excellent books and systems for promoting effective time management. Different personality styles also respond to different systems but you'll definitely need some sort of time-management system.[139] There's even an online system that you can use for free.[140]

Portfolio workers are recognisable because they usually carry with them a diary and 'to do' system, be it electronic, paper or in the clouds of the Internet. In some form or another, they've calendars that mirror their complicated lifestyles. And they've lists of people who provide them with the range of support they need. One of their biggest challenges is to ensure that these systems work for them instead of dictating to them.

CAN DO: How are you managing your time right now?

It's not unusual for us to spend huge amounts of time analysing returns and pay-offs from our investments, working out the 'best buy' for a freezer, DVD or brand of marmalade, or spending hours bidding on eBay. Yet, quite often, we fail to transfer these considerable analytical skills to our own lives.

It can be very valuable to reflect regularly on:

- **How much time am I selling (getting paid for or preparing to get paid for), how much time am I doing basic maintenance and how much discretionary time do I have?**

- What returns am I getting for the time and energy I'm investing?
- What parts of my life are my 'best buys'?
- How am I actually filling the hours of each day?
- What would it be good to change?

We know from research into weight control that most of us are notoriously unreliable when it comes to recalling what we eat and the same is true for how we spend our time. Consequently, we invite you to keep a record of your activities for what you think is a fairly typical week of your life.

The best way to do this is to record what you've done at the end of each day. Fill in your time-log like the table provided here.

	am						pm					
	2:00	4:00	6:00	8:00	10:00	12:00	14:00	16:00	18:00	20:00	22:00	24:00
Monday												
Tuesday												
Wednesday												
Thursday												
Friday												
Saturday												
Sunday												

At the end of the week ask yourself these questions.

How typical was this week?

_____

_____

_____

_____

What does this snapshot tell me about the way I'm spending my time?

_____

_____

_____

_____

How much of my week was spent doing things I choose to do?

_____

_____

_____

_____

What might I want to change?

_____

_____

_____

_____

What are the most rewarding activities I do that I'd like to do more of?

_____

_____

_____

_____

What are the least rewarding activities that I'd like to do less of?

_____

_____

_____

_____

After you've completed your time-log for a week, study it and, using three differently coloured markers, highlight each item according to whether it was **sold**, **maintenance** or **discretionary** time.[141]

Sold time is the time you sell to an employer. It involves exchanging your time for money. It extends beyond the actual hours spent doing paid work because it includes time spent in preparing for work, travelling to work and attending events related to work. It will also include learning and training time and networking – activities we do in the hope that they'll translate into income at some point.

Maintenance time is the time spent keeping things ticking over. It includes sleeping, eating, shopping, cooking, cleaning, etc. It also includes maintaining others – your partner, children, parents and so on.

Discretionary time is the time that remains. It's when you choose what you want to do.

Having completed your colouring exercise, now add up the hours that you've spent under each heading. When you look at your results is there anything that surprises you? Does this suggest changes that you might like to make as to how you're investing your time?

Most of us want to increase our discretionary time. Write down below what you might do to be able to achieve this.

_____

_____

_____

_____

People we interviewed have suggested things like:

- cutting down on watching TV;
- travelling by train instead of car to get more things done;
- checking e-mails only once or twice a day;
- getting other members of the household to share tasks;
- hiring people to help out with, for example, cleaning, getting children to and from school, DIY, doing the accounts, etc.
- minding the gap – deliberately schedule some gaps for your discretionary time and don't fill them unless there's a real emergency.

In theory, new technology should help us enormously – but does it?

'If technology is as good as I think, then why am I always so tired? The problem isn't lack of sleep. It's lack of dreams. I've become so efficient, I no longer have time to daydream. When a new product or service cuts 45 minutes off the time to complete a task, we don't enjoy a nap. Instead, we cram an extra assignment into the day.'
Noreen Seebacher[142]

Benjamin Ellis[143] suggests that you do the following. List the things you:

- don't want to do and actually don't need to do.
- don't want to do but actually need to do.
- want to do and actually need to do.
- want to do but actually don't need to do.

Each has its own particular challenges.

Jim Collins[144] suggests you have a 'stop-doing' list as well as your to-do list.

Try this for yourself. List the things you should stop doing NOW.

_____

_____

_____

_____

Steve Jobs, the founder of Apple and Pixar, revealed that a 'stop-doing' strategy was key to Apple's approach: 'People think focus means saying yes to the thing you've got to focus on. But that's not what it means at all. It means saying no to the hundred other good ideas that there are. You have to pick carefully. I'm actually as proud of many of the things we haven't done as the things we have done.'

Can you think of at least one thing that you are proud that you never did?

Sometimes the danger with a portfolio career is that you really do think that you can do it all. Remember that you can do anything, but not _everything_.

Managing your energy

Energy is hugely important for people with portfolio careers. Some people have naturally high energy, but one area which we both feel is often overlooked is the energy we receive or that's sapped from us by other people and outside influencers such as the media.

As a broadcast news journalist, Katie used to read, listen and inwardly dissect every last detail and nuance of 'the news'. She was taught how to quickly find the negative and 'yes, but' in every so-called story. Now don't get us wrong, challenging a government minister who's being economical with the truth is a useful and correct action to take. But deliberately setting out to take someone down a peg or two just because you can seems a bit like a waste of energy and indeed creates _negative_ energy.

When Katie left the newsroom after 12 years, she tried an experiment with some new (self-imposed) rules.

1 No news radio when first waking. Wait 10 to 15 minutes before tuning in.

2 Stop watching TV – in reality, she allowed about 10 hours a year plus very occasional viewing online.

3 She started reading interesting and informative blogs.

The experiment was so successful, in terms of increased positive energy and creating time to focus on her real passions, that nearly four years later, Katie's still doing it.

Mike Pegg[145] talks about 'drillers' and 'fillers'. He asks you to imagine that your energy is in a pot. Each time we engage with people we enjoy and who challenge us in a good way, they fill our pot with energy. Each time we engage with people who like to complain and moan, they drill little holes in our pot and the energy quickly drains away.

Who are the fillers and drillers in your life?

Can you find a way to spend more time with the fillers and less with the drillers? What elements of your life fill and drill your pot?

Barrie, similarly, talks about 'emotional black holes.' These are people who just suck up your energy and give nothing back. Avoid them.

Managing pressure and stress

A portfolio career isn't a career choice for the faint hearted. And it's certainly not an attractive option for those who like to move and think slowly.

'It's not an either/or situation. I can have a bit of being a parent and have a career and enjoy it as long as it remains in my control – I'm a flexi-mum. It's a second chance for me. Many people don't get a chance to find out what they really want to do.' Karen Cannard

'I was scared and out of my comfort zone. Was I employable over the age of 50? I didn't appreciate the skills I had built up over the years. I now have eight jobs, earn almost double what I used to earn and have flexibility, variety and a better social life. The only thing I had to get used to was working on my own a lot. Now I don't think I could work any other way'. Trish Cowie

You may well work primarily on your own and not be part of a team – this is commented on quite often by our respondents. On the other hand, they wouldn't change it at all. Below are some of the classic ways of helping to manage pressure in your life.

- **Look after your physical well-being.**
- **Get enough sleep.**
- **Learn to relax.**
- **Keep to a regular routine.**

- Know others who can help you.
- Don't blame or punish yourself.
- Manage your decisions one at a time.

Look after your physical well-being

Your ability to cope with stress depends on your physical well-being. Everyone needs to be fit and well to cope with a portfolio career, so exercise and eating regularly and wisely are essential coping skills. We found it interesting how many of our interviewees have clearly designed physical regimes to fight stress and overload. They quoted yoga, regular exercise, go to the gym, run, walk, ride, swim, ski, even regular sex. Some – though a minority – did take many short holidays.

'If I had less to do that would be really stressful!.' Zulfi Hussein

One of the things that we know about exercise is that it has now clearly been demonstrated that it improves creativity and overall cognitive performance.[146] It also produces endorphins, which militate against stress and just makes you feel good.

'One of the things I love about this work style is that it gives me time to train for triathlons and these, of course, keep me fit for the demanding work pattern that I have chosen.' Lisa Milnor

Katie catches up on background reading on her treadmill. Barrie sometimes has business meetings while running, although he mostly runs for fun – honestly!

Anthropologists reckon that prehistoric humans covered about 12 miles a day. As John Medina puts it, 'That means our fancy brains developed not while we were lounging about but while we were working out'.[147]

Get enough sleep

Portfolio workers often display high energy levels and many of us can exhibit a rather 'macho' attitude towards sleep.

Well, do we have some news for you! All of the research on sleep suggests that although clearly there are large individual differences, most of us really do need seven to eight hours' sleep a night for maximum overall health and for efficient and creative brain use. The researchers are still arguing as to why we need to sleep but they're in agreement about how necessary it is. What we *do* know is that although your body may be at rest, your brain is still active and appears to need that period to accomplish a range of restorative functions. William Dement, one of the pioneers of sleep research, when asked about the function of dreaming, said, 'Dreaming permits each and every one of us to be quietly and safely insane every night of our lives.' As a portfolio worker, are you doing enough to encourage your nightly insanity?

We've already discussed the owl versus lark dichotomy but there's also the issue about napping. If you've more control over how you spend your time, then in theory you might also benefit from a mid-afternoon nap. John Medina[147] calls it the 'nap zone', a period of time in the mid-afternoon when we experience transient sleepiness. The Mediterranean concept of a siesta actually institutionalises this. At first, scientists thought this was simply a product of sleep deprivation but now there's a growing consensus that a long sleep at night and a mid-afternoon nap might just represent human sleep behaviour at its most natural. NASA has shown that a 26-minute nap improved a pilot's performance by more than 34 per cent. And a 45-minute nap produced a similar increase in cognitive performance which lasted more than six hours.

We also know that if healthy 30 year olds are sleep deprived for six days (in this study about four hours of sleep a night), parts of their body chemistry resembled that of a 60 year old. It also took them a week of normal sleep to get back to their 30-year-old state.

Are you getting the picture? Lack of sleep affects attention, executive function, working memory, mood, quantitative skills, logical reasoning, motor efficiency and creativity. So sleep as much as you need to feel rested and alert the next day and take a nap if you need to.

Learn to relax

Relaxation techniques are well worth learning, as they can help prevent you from becoming too uptight about things that are bothering you. Make a point of spending a little time relaxing each day. Again, high-energy people sometimes appear to take pride in not needing to relax. But if you do relax, then you're more likely to retain your high energy.

It can sometimes help to give yourself a treat too: an outing to a favourite peaceful spot; a visit to the hairdresser or to a friend; or buying yourself something small that you'll enjoy. And, of course, how about a holiday now and then?

If you're lucky, you may even have a portfolio career that contributes directly to your relaxation.

Nick Beadle, a Reiki practitioner as well as photographer and lighting designer, says: 'Reiki works for yourself as well as for your clients'.

Nick and his partner, Annie, spent a long time searching for the house that would accommodate both of their portfolio careers and reckon that this has made their lives considerably less stressful.

'We've bought a home specifically to house our two careers. We needed two rooms that we could use for photography and for Reiki. Annie is also now trained in Reiki and will run the photography business. She'll continue to do her freelance HR work in Cumbria (they live near Nottingham). She's usually away for about four days at a time when she does that. I'm usually away for about a week when I'm doing my theatre work. '

For Nick and Annie, their home is clearly an 'anchor point'.

Keep to a regular routine

Routine and structure in your life can be of great assistance in times of pressure. Look for the 'anchor points' in your life, the stable areas that remain the same even when everything else is changing. These can include your basic routines, such as going to bed or eating at a regular hour, shopping or working outside or in the home.

Spending time with special people can be a lifeline during stressful periods. But again there are huge individual differences. Barrie knew a high-flying CEO of a major company who was constantly travelling from country to country. In answer to Barrie's question as to how he coped with all of this change, he replied that no matter what country he was in he always demanded to be served a full English breakfast with brown toast and proper marmalade. In fact, he always took his own marmalade with him as no brand other than Coopers Oxford Thick Marmalade would do.

Some people who are largely running a business from home love the fact that they can be in a dressing gown until lunchtime. Others, even if they don't have to meet face to face with clients, have to be available from early in the day and they like to put on 'work clothes' as soon as they get up.

'It's a signal to me and to the children that I am now in work mode just as if I were going out to a job.' Heather Jackson

Knowing others who can help

There's now considerable evidence to show that talking problems through with people helps to reduce stress at times of change. Having a support group is a valuable asset. Your own support group could include your partner, parents, relatives, friends and so on. It's important to develop a range of 'helpers' rather than being dependent on just one or two people for everything. That's why we've devoted a whole Step in this book to this subject alone.

Don't blame or punish yourself

When things go wrong, as they're bound to sometimes, don't waste time in destructive self-criticism. This just undermines your self-esteem even further. Take time out to think about the new situation and how best to deal with it. Give yourself a little treat to boost your feelings and you'll be surprised how much easier it is to deal with whatever you feel has gone wrong. Ask yourself what you've learned from the situation. See our section on managing 'failure'.

Manage your decisions one at a time

It's surprising how many decisions can be safely postponed until you feel better able to make them. This isn't the same as letting events or other people make your decisions for you, or dodging the whole issue and putting it off indefinitely. Rather, it's the clever knack of recognising which decisions have the highest priority and must be dealt with now and which decisions can safely wait until you've more information, or until a decision has become absolutely necessary.

Don't let other people push you into making a decision that you don't feel ready to make. If necessary, tell yourself and other people that you're busy dealing with another decision which must come first, and that you'll deal with the next one when you're ready. This is called 'planned procrastination'. It's very different from actual procrastination, even if it might look the same to an observer.

Managing transitions and change

John Lennon said that, 'Life is what happens to you when you are busy making plans'. There are many things and events in life that we can predict but there are others that take us by surprise and can have a dramatic impact on your portfolio career: marriage, redundancy, divorce, pregnancy, bereavement, etc. Less dramatic but still demanding could be a car accident, illness in the family or support system or even being ill yourself, power cuts which mean computers don't work, bad weather preventing travel and so on.

Portfolio workers probably have to manage more transitions than people who have other career patterns. Each time we change our portfolio we have a transition to manage. But change is not the same as a transition.

- **Change** is what happens *to us* – the external.
- **Transition** is how we deal with it – the internal.

A change can happen quite quickly but its impact – the transition – may take and often does take longer. Changes can be frequent and minor. A transition can be life changing.

If you've a good understanding of how transitions have an impact on you, you'll be much better equipped to deal with them. We want to introduce a model of transitions[148] to help you understand how they affect you. If you can understand the process of a transition, you'll manage it more effectively.

Knowing where you are on the transition curve (see page 218) and knowing that you can manage the process when it hits you can help you move through the transition more easily. Many people think they can jump across some of the steps on the curve but the research tells us they're kidding themselves. You may feel that you've moved on but if you haven't faced up to the full range of feelings that accompanied the transition then most likely the whole process will blow up in your face and you'll have to step backwards to catch up.

Our feelings, during a transition, tend to go through seven stages. It's important to remember that we'll need to go through all seven stages of the transition curve before the process is complete. Some of the stages may be very brief, but we still have to go through them in one form or another.

The seven stages of transition

After reading each explanation, try to remember a time when you were in a transition and have felt like that.

Changes in self-esteem during transitions

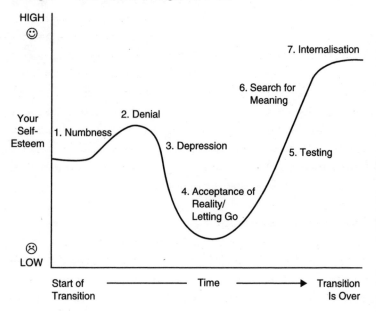

1 Numbness

The first phase is sometimes described as shock. It's a sense of being overwhelmed, of being unable to make plans, unable to reason and unable to understand. In other words, you freeze up. The more unfamiliar the transition, the stronger this feeling is. In bereavement, for example, many people feel strange because of the absence of feeling but it's normal to feel numb at this stage of a transition. However, if you feel positive about a transition – getting married, for example, or landing a new job – this stage will be less intense.

2 Denial

The movement from numbness to denial, the second stage, doesn't feel greatly different at the time it's happening. This is because we try to make the transition seem less important or argue that it won't affect us. Very often, we'll attempt to deny that a transition even exists.

During this stage people may feel, 'This isn't as bad as I expected' or that 'Things will soon be back to normal.' This is often because the body is building up its defences for the full impact of the change, which is yet to come. At this stage, the person may feel highly energetic because, with a transition like redundancy, the person is often at the centre of attention from their friends and relatives, plus there are things to be done and to be dealt with. With a change such as a new job, the denial stage may be a refusal to recognise some of the real changes that will take place, for example the loss of workmates, taking on new responsibilities and the uncertainty about being able to do the new job.

3 Depression/self-doubt

For most people, the realities of the transition – and of the stress that comes with it – will eventually begin to become clear. As people become aware that they must make some changes in the way they're living, as they become aware of the realities involved, they sometimes become uncertain. Self-doubt is usually a consequence of feelings of powerlessness, of aspects of life being out of our control. This can happen even when we're really looking forward to a change, not only when it's feared. So, getting that dream job, for example, can lead to doubts about being capable of doing the job.

In this stage, the person can have periods of high energy, which can sometimes show itself as anger, before sliding back into a feeling of hopelessness. They may become frustrated because it seems difficult to know how best to cope with the new life situation, the new ways of being and the new relationships that have been established.

4 Letting go

As people gradually become aware of their reality, they can move into the fourth phase, letting go, which can be a gradual 'three steps forward – two steps back' type of process. Someone who has left an unsatisfying job may feel she has let go of it but then sees her ex-colleagues again socially. This may be quite painful and makes her think: 'This is awful. I thought I had moved on but I really haven't'.

To move from phase three to phase four involves a process of unhooking from the past and saying 'Well, here I am now, this is what I have and I know I can survive. I may not be sure of what I want yet, but I will be OK.' Once the new reality or situation has been accepted the person begins to feel optimistic.

5 Testing

The person becomes much more active and starts testing him or herself in the new situation, trying out new behaviours and new ways of coping with the change. After losing a really valued job, this is often the stage when people begin actively networking again. There's a lot of personal energy available during this phase and it sometimes shows itself in irritation or tears. It can often be a very testing time for the person's friends, too, as each day a different 'self' can appear.

6 Search for meaning

Following this burst of activity and self-testing, there's a gradual shift towards self-questioning, when the person may ask, 'Is this right for me?' or 'What does this mean for me?' We need to know what the changes mean to us and how they'll affect our future. If the change is not 'right for us', then there'll be further testing of alternatives until one is found that seems to fit. It's only when we've a sense of what these changes mean, and what their meaning for our life is, that we can move on to the final stage.

7 Internalisation

At last, if we've been able to accept the transition, we move into the final phase of internalisation. This is when we take all the effects of the transition and make them part of our lives or routines. When we've fully accepted (internalised) the stages of the transition that we've been through, then we can begin to look forward in a more positive frame of mind and start to build on the new strengths we've developed.

Rarely, if ever, does a person move neatly from phase to phase. For example, one person may never get beyond denial. Another may just stop at depression. But, for a transition to be effectively managed, all seven phases need to be worked through. Often we try to avoid the depression stage, or help others avoid it, but when we allow ourselves or others to grieve we can move towards the new opportunities opened up to us by the change.

Understanding the process of change and the stages of transition will help you to cope with your feelings and move forward.

Tips for managing your transitions

Life is a series of challenges for each of us, whether we like it or not. Some people enjoy stability and like things to remain constant. Others are only happy when we're on the move. Many people are afraid of change and transitions. But transitions are not all negative. Many of them are extremely enjoyable or have positive results. Even transitions which appear negative on the surface can turn out to be enjoyable or at least valuable learning experiences.

So, the first trick of good transition management is to learn to look on every transition, every challenge, not as a potential problem but as an opportunity to make something positive happen in your life.

It sometimes helps you to face your fears by asking 'What's the worst thing that can happen?' Our anxieties are usually based upon vague and fantastic fears. Actually facing up to the worst that can happen may help us to identify possibilities. If we think and talk about these possibilities, we'll probably find that they're not that terrible, or that they're unlikely to happen. Even if the worst does happen, at least we've prepared ourselves for it.

All transitions involve making decisions: sometimes easy, sometimes painful. Letting other people make decisions for you doesn't help you to manage your transition and grow in the ways that you want. However, there are a number of things you can do which can help you be more proactive and feel more in control. They include all of the mechanisms that we quoted earlier to manage pressure and stress, but it adds to the list two crucial directives:

• Manage your transitions one at a time.
• Remember that time will help but time needs a hand.

Manage your transitions one at a time
Many of us are tempted to change everything in one go. Sheila got divorced and decided that this was the time to sell the house, start a portfolio career and move. Unless you have to, this is definitely not a good idea and the research on life changes and health strongly support this.

Remember that time will help but time needs a hand
Time will help you come to terms with any new situation. But in order to come through a transition feeling that you have learned from the experience, you need to help yourself along the way. All of the reading and the thinking that you're doing now will help you to manage the transition in a proactive way – for yourself.

Learning from 'failures'
'I have not failed. I've just found 999 ways that won't work.'
Thomas Edison

We prefer to use the word 'setbacks' instead of 'failure'. However, it's a term commonly used and one that often has dire psychological consequences for people who use it, which is why we've put it in inverted commas here. The word 'failure' is normally used pejoratively. Rarely can it be used descriptively as almost always it's someone's opinion. And almost always what we really mean is that something that we have tried hasn't worked out. That is the be all and end all of it. Yet sadly we then label the experience as a failure and all too often broaden that out to state that we are a failure. We believe strongly that we wouldn't get far in life without some things going wrong for us. The challenge is to ensure that we learn from what went wrong. The early promoter of self-help, Samuel Smiles, put it elegantly at the turn of the 20th century:

'We learn wisdom from failure much more than from success. We often discover what will do, by finding out what will not do; and probably he who never made a mistake never made a discovery.'

JK Rowling made a wonderful speech at Harvard University[149] in which she expounded on the benefits of failure:

'Failure gave me an inner security that I had never attained by passing examinations. Failure taught me things about myself that I could have learned no other way. I discovered that I had a strong will and more discipline than I had suspected; I also found out that I had friends whose value was truly above rubies.

The knowledge that you have emerged wiser and stronger from setbacks means that you are, ever after, secure in your ability to survive. You will never truly know yourself, or the strength of your relationships, until both have been tested by adversity. Such knowledge is a true gift, for all that it is painfully won, and it has been worth more to me than any qualification I ever earned.'

We love the words of legendary basketball player Michael Jordan:

'I've missed more than 9,000 shots in my career. I've lost almost 300 games. Twenty-six times I've been trusted to take the game-winning shot – and missed. I've failed over and over and over again in my life. And that is why I succeed.'[150]

There's even an online publication in the US devoted to failure **(www.failuremag.com)**. As you'll see, it's a bit tongue in cheek!

So why are we especially emphasising the importance of managing failure to portfolio career workers? Simply because many of them have told us about experiences that didn't work out, plans that went awry, contracts that were withdrawn. This can happen to anyone, of course, but the very nature of having a portfolio of jobs can multiply the chances of having to deal with this more often than might be the case for a single-track or serial careerist.

This is simply another way of making the point that there can be great risks in pursuing a portfolio career. But remember, there are also considerable risks in having all of one's career eggs in one organisational basket. Without risks what do we have?

'But there is suffering in life, and there are defeats. No one can avoid them. But it's better to lose some of the battles in the struggles for your dreams than to be defeated without ever knowing what you're fighting for.' Paulo Coelho

And in similar vein, George Bernard Shaw's comment that, 'A life spent making mistakes is not only more honourable but more useful than a life spent in doing nothing'.

CAN DO: What I've learned from my 'failures'

Think back to what you remember as your greatest failure in your school or college days. Write it down here: _____

Now do the same for your paid work life. Write it down here:

_____

_____

And finally, for your personal life outside of paid work. Write it down here:

_____

_____

For each of these in turn, reflect hard and come up with at least one thing that you've learned in retrospect from each of these failures. Write them down.

School/college days _____

Work _____

Personal _____

Now these, of course, are very big events in your life. But many days will have small failures as part of the texture of life and the occasional day will have a much bigger failure. The trick is to develop the habit of asking yourself after one of the bigger failures has occurred:

- What I have I learned as a result of this?
- How might I do this differently in the future?
- What's the worst thing that could have happened? And did it?

There's a Chinese proverb which simply says that failure is not about falling down but about refusing to get up:

'The never-ending journey...Learning and developing'.

Just as meaningful work is crucial to our humanity, so is learning. Work and learning are inextricably tied together. A common thread to be found with successful people is that they never stop learning. They're like TV reporters and five-year-old children. They have an insatiable curiosity. They want to know stuff. They're driven to understand the world and they ask a lot of questions.

'All you need in this life is ignorance and confidence, and then success is sure'. Mark Twain

CAN DO: What have I learned today?

Think about what's happened in your day so far. Can you think of at least one thing that you've learned today? It might be a skill, it might be some new information, it might be a new point of view. Write it down. If you're an owl and nothing much has happened yet, review what happened yesterday.

_____

_____

_____

_____

'I think you need a shed at the end of your garden. You have to find a way of getting personal space to work.' Richard Maude

Learning, life-long learning, is an essential skill. Many of us were born into a generation where we hared our way through school, and for the privileged few, university. A learning sprint, then work. The pace of change in society and business, and the speed at which new knowledge is being created, means that's no longer sufficient. Learning must now be a life-long process.

Sometimes learning will make us feel awkward and unskilled but that's simply the first stage of learning something new. NLP practitioners[151] refer to four stages of learning.

- The first is when we're **unconsciously incompetent.**
- The second is when we're **consciously incompetent.**
- The third is when we're **consciously competent.**
- And the fourth is when we're **unconsciously competent.**

When you first sit behind the steering wheel of a car, you feel almost total incompetence. Once you've had lessons and have passed your test, you're able to drive. You can't even remember the journey as you've have been thinking of other things and the driving is automatic. You've become unconsciously competent.

'Move out of your comfort zone. You can only grow if you're willing to feel awkward and uncomfortable when you try something new.' Brian Tracy

Learn to love new technology

Throughout this book we've written a great deal about the effective use of technology. This is a crucial life skill for everyone no matter what their chosen career pattern. For portfolio workers, it's even more crucial. How else will you be able to manage your complicated timetable, call on your support systems, network, market yourself, build your brand and tell your stories?

Portfolio workers must use technology to survive. This applies to all workers but especially to those who continually change their jobs, add a new job to their work portfolio or branch out in variety of new directions. What it means to be successful at work is changing and much of the new wave is focused on tapping factual knowledge. Research conducted by Dr Robert Kelley of Carnegie Mellon University asked workers: 'what percentage of the knowledge you need to do your job is stored in your mind? The answers have varied significantly over the last 20 plus years. In 1986, it was 75 per cent, then in 1997 (the year the Internet began to take off in the business world), the answer was 15-20 per cent. In 2008, it was 8-10 per cent. Imagine how a manager will answer this question in 2012?

If we were to lose our smartphones, access to the Internet, the software that we use daily and e-mail, we might still be able to pursue portfolio careers but it would certainly be a lot more stressful. So we always advise people to keep up to date with new developments in technology. Your software might be replaced by the 'cloud', your website by your blog, your meetings by video conferencing or hologramatic events and who knows what else in the years to come. Stay alert to new possibilities. Enjoy learning about them. Play with them.

Summary
You've:

- recapped on your learning so far;
- speculated on your future – or at least the next five years;
- explored how best to manage your time and work flow;
- looked at ways of managing pressure and stress;
- examined the seven stages of managing a transition;
- learned from things that haven't worked out for you – what some people call 'failure';
- acquired an understanding of why it's vital for you to continually learn and develop;
- acquired an appreciation of why you always need to keep abreast of new technologies.

Notes

138 John Medina, *Brain Rules* (Pear Press, 2008).

139 Barrie Hopson and Mike Scally, *Time Management: Conquer the Clock* (Mercury, 1991); Clare Evans, *Time Management for Dummies* (UK edition, Wiley, 2008); Pamela Dodd and Doug Sundheim, *The 25 Best Time Management Tools and Techniques: How to Get More Done without Driving Yourself Crazy* (Capstone, 2008).

140 **www.rescuetime.com**

141 This classification of time was developed by Jack Loughary of the University of Oregon with whom Barrie worked in the 1980s.

142 **Blog: http://globestrealtybytes.wordpress.com**

143 **http://redcatco.com/blog/productivity/watch-out-for-the-frogs/**

144 Quoted in Matthew May's book, *In Pursuit of Elegance: Why the Best Ideas Have Something Missing* (Broadway Business, 2009).

145 Mike is keen to point out that the original concept of 'drillers' and 'fillers' was created by Virginia Satir, a family therapist, in her book, *Peoplemaking* (Souvenir Press, 1990).

146 John Medina, *Brain Rules* (Pear Press, 2008).

147 Ibid.

148 John Adams, John Hayes, Barrie Hopson, *Understanding and Managing Transitions* (Martin Robertson, 1976).

149 **http://tinyurl.com/c9m36f**

150 **http://tinyurl.com/2go4sx**

151 Neurolinguistic programming

Final Thoughts

today i will
experience
joy.

This book has been a labour of love in many ways. It's given us the privilege of talking and meeting with some extraordinary people, people who are creating portfolio careers that blend with the whole of their lives, and which allow them to be all they can be and want to be. They are people who've been guided by their values and learned to rely on that 'old-fashioned' sense of intuition, people who've refused to play the straight 9 to 5 corporate game. We thank you and applaud you for your time, honesty and willingness to share your stories and experience.

You may have read this book and thought, 'I'd love to try that **but**…'

And you'll find a whole host of reasons why you shouldn't do it. Yes, it can be scary. It can make you appear 'different'. You might frighten your parents, family and friends. But, what we've discovered is that it can also generate admiration and great curiousity.

We may have described 10 Steps but reading this book is actually the very first one. It's what you choose to do from here that's the real journey and the one during which, we hope, you'll learn, grow and enjoy being all you want to and can possibly be. Please don't waste time comparing yourself with others. There will always be people who are cleverer, quicker, more attractive and earn more than you do. Get over it. Because it doesn't matter. What *does* matter is that you become the best you can be. And that's different for all of us.

'Be a first-rate version of yourself, not a second-rate version of someone else.' Judy Garland

Nick Williams[152] sums it up rather well:

'I would like to reinvent the idea of a proper job: it has many strands, a portfolio; its hours suit our lifestyle; it allows us to find and utilise the best and most creative parts of us; it incorporates and accommodates us as a whole person; it affords the opportunity to grow, expand and discover more about ourselves; it is based on win–win and co-operation; it allows us to expand into being a whole human being – mind, body, emotions and spirit. That is proper work!'

In reinventing yourself, one final plea: whatever you choose to do, let your passions fuel it and your skills drive it. And most importantly, remember to enjoy your journey.

Note

152 *The Work We Were Born To Do* (Element Books, 2007).

Resources

FREELANCING
www.freelanceuk.com/become/is_freelancing_for_me.shtml
www.freelancers.net/
www.bcs.org/server.php?show=nav.7955
www.futurenet.com/jobs/stdTemplate.aspx/Jobs_In_Publishing/
Freelancing This is largely for writing and editing jobs.
www.xchangeteam.com/
www.pcg.org.uk/cms/index.php

For a free guide to freelancing go to
www.freelanceadvisor.co.uk/2009/02/26/go-freelance-the-guide-to-starting-freelancing/
Flexitimers at **www.flexitimers.com/flexible-future/labels/Flexitimers.html**

RATE FOR THE JOB
www.peopleperhour.com/
www.ifreelance.com/ This is largely for the US but UK jobs also come up.
www.creativepro.com/article/the-art-of-business-negotiating-fees
http://selfemployment.suite101.com/article.cfm/negotiating_fees_and_contracts

THE LEGAL SIDE OF FREELANCING
www.self-employed.uk.com/default.asp
Also, of course, just Google 'freelance' or 'freelancing' as new sites come up all the time.

Setting up your own business

And in particular if you want to start up your business from home, register with **www.enterprisenation.com.** The site is a goldmine for people starting up any new business. Enterprise Nation has also bought out a guide to working 5–9. This can be downloaded free from its website.

Networking

Download the free networking assessment tool from UpMo at **www.upmo.com/profiler.** On the site you you'll also find some downloadable letter templates for 'getting reconnected', finding a job through networking, and a thank-you response. Particularly interesting is their free downloadable research report 'Professional Networking and Its Impact on Career Advancement: A Study of Practices, Systems and Opinions of High-Earning, Elite Professionals'.

Using redundancy to help set up your portfolio career

Go to **www.moneysavingexpert.com/protect/redundancy-help** where there's an excellent checklist that takes you through all aspects of redundancy.

Appendix **Value cards**

PROMOTION
You like to work where
there's a good chance of
promotion and aspire to
high achievement.
Score __

HELPING SOCIETY
You like to think that
your work will make
a contribution to the
community, society or
the world.
Score __

A WELL-KNOWN
ORGANISATION
You like being part of a
well-known organisation.
Score __

ARTISTIC
You appreciate art,
music, design, books,
theatre, film, etc.
Score __

PLACE OF WORK
Where you work is
important to you.
Score __

STATUS
You prize being held
in high esteem for
your qualities and
achievements.
Score __

5	Very important
4	Important
3	Quite important
2	Of some importance
1	Not important

VALUE
CARDS

VALUE
CARDS

VALUE
CARDS

VALUE
CARDS

VALUE
CARDS

VALUE
CARDS

WORK–LIFE BLEND
You want a balance
between your paid work
and all the other areas
of your life.
Score __

PRECISE WORK
You like working at
things that involve great
care and concentration.
Score __

FRIENDSHIP
You would or do like
close relationships
with the people you
work with.
Score __

SECURITY
You like to know that
your work will always be
there for you.
Score __

CONTACT WITH
PEOPLE
You enjoy having a lot of
contact and interaction
with people.
Score __

TEAMWORK
You like working with
others and collective
achievement.
Score __

5	Very important
4	Important
3	Quite important
2	Of some importance
1	Not important

VALUE CARDS	VALUE CARDS
VALUE CARDS	VALUE CARDS
VALUE CARDS	VALUE CARDS

EXCITEMENT
You need a lot
of excitement in
your life.
Score ___

MAKING DECISIONS
You like making
decisions about how
things should be done,
who should do it and
by when.
Score ___

PHYSICAL
CHALLENGE
You enjoy doing
something that's
physically demanding.
Score ___

PRESSURE
You like working
to deadlines and a
fast pace.
Score ___

SUPERVISION
You enjoy being
responsible for work
done by others.
Score ___

CHALLENGE
You like being stretched
and given new problems
to work on.
Score ___

5 Very important
4 Important
3 Quite important
2 Of some importance
1 Not important

VALUE CARDS

VALUE CARDS

VALUE CARDS

VALUE CARDS

VALUE CARDS

VALUE CARDS

INDEPENDENCE
You like being
independent, a free
agent, in charge of your
own life and options.
Score __

BEING EXPERT
You like being known as
someone with special
knowledge or skills.
Score __

MONEY
It matters to you to have
a healthy bank balance
and significant assets.
Score __

HELPING OTHERS
You like to help other
people individually or in
groups as part of
your work.
Score __

LEARNING
It's important to you to
continually learn
new things.
Score __

PERSUADING PEOPLE
You enjoy persuading
people to change
their minds, buy
something, volunteer
for something, etc.
Score __

5	Very important
4	Important
3	Quite important
2	Of some importance
1	Not important

VALUE CARDS

VALUE CARDS

VALUE CARDS

VALUE CARDS

VALUE CARDS

VALUE CARDS

ROUTINE
You prefer a work
routine that's fairly
predictable.
Score __

COMMUNICATION
You enjoy being able
to express ideas well in
writing or in speech.
Score __

RISK
You like to take physical,
financial, emotional or
intellectual risks.
Score __

TIME FREEDOM
You prefer to be able to
choose your own times
for doing things.
Score __

PEACE
You prefer to have
few pressures or
uncomfortable demands.
Score __

CREATIVE
Thinking up new
ideas and ways of
doing, expressing or
representing things is
important to you.
Score __

5	Very important
4	Important
3	Quite important
2	Of some importance
1	Not important

VALUE CARDS

VALUE CARDS

VALUE CARDS

VALUE CARDS

VALUE CARDS

COMPETITION
You like competing against other people or groups.
Score ___

MY ADDITIONAL VALUE

VARIETY
You like to have lots of different things to do and frequent change.
Score ___

MY ADDITIONAL VALUE

MY ADDITIONAL VALUE

About Hugh MacLeod

Hugh MacLeod is a cartoonist, who makes his living publishing fine art prints via the Internet. See: **www.gapingvoidgallery.com**

Hugh is also well known for his ideas about how Web 2.0 affects advertising and marketing. After a decade of working as an advertising copywriter, Hugh started blogging at gapingvoid.com in 2001. He began by publishing his cartoons but as time wore on he started blogging about his other main interest: marketing.

In 2004, he wrote 'Ignore Everybody' **(http://www.gapingvoid. com/Moveable_Type/archives/000932.html)** and 'The Hughtrain' **(http://hughtrain.com)**, both of which were widely read in the blogosphere and downloaded over a million times in total.

In 2005, he scored his first major blog marketing success with EnglishCut.com, a blog he started with Savile Row tailor, Thomas Mahon. It tripled Thomas's sales within six months. Since mid-2006, Hugh has also been helping a small South African winery, Stormhoek

(Stormhoek.com), to 'rise above the clutter' in the wine market by using Web 2.0 tools to get the word out. Sales have gone up fivefold during that time.

Since 2006, Hugh has been constantly engaged as a public speaker, giving talks in both Europe and the US, talking about Web 2.0 and the ramifications it has on business.

Hugh's basic mantra about blog marketing is 'Blogs are a good way to make things happen indirectly', a point lost on many corporate types.

His new book is *Ignore Everybody: And 39 Other Keys to Creativity* (Portfolio, 2009).

E-mail: **gapingvoid@gmail.com**
Blog: **www.gapingvoid.com**
Gallery: **www.gapingvoidgallery.com**

About the authors

Dr Barrie Hopson's portfolio includes...being chairman of Axia Interactive Media, a non-executive director of two other companies, writer, presenter, consultant and chair of his local community association. He has a long history of involvement in the area of career development. He established the Counselling and Career Development Unit at Leeds University in 1976 and subsequently went on to found Lifeskills International.

Barrie has written 38 books including the bestselling *12 Steps to Success through Service, The Lifeskills Teaching Programmes and Build Your Own Rainbow*. His most recent book is *The Rainbow Years: the Pluses of Being 50+* and an accompanying website **http://tinyurl.com/mmpdt2**. The latter were all co-authored with Mike Scally. Barrie has worked widely as a consultant to commercial and educational organisations in the UK, US, Asia, Canada and Europe. He is married with two grown-up children, two small but disarming grandchildren and sees one of the major payoffs of his portfolio career as being able to follow Yorkshire County Cricket Club.

Katie Ledger's portfolio includes...being a communications coach, visual storyteller, conference facilitator and producer, author and TV reporter for BBC Click. She helps people, teams and organisations to communicate in a compelling way that has a high impact on audiences.

Katie spent 12 years working as a news presenter for Five News, ITN and the BBC. Currently, she works in companies such as Microsoft, MSN, Sony, Reed Elsevier, 3 Mobile, Wiley Publishing, Waterstone's, the Post Office and the Police Federation. She's therefore well equipped to cope with the high-pressure situations she regularly faces dealing with two small children, two cats, one husband and a very busy but fulfilling work style. She writes a portfolio careers blog with Barrie at **www.portfoliocareers.net**.

Index